THE SILENCING OF GOD

THE DISMANTLING OF AMERICA'S CHRISTIAN HERITAGE

DAVE MILLER, PH.D

Apologetics Press, Inc.

230 Landmark Drive

Montgomery, Alabama 36117-2752

© Copyright 2008
ISBN: 978-1-60063-018-7

The Silencing of God:
        The Dismantling of America's Christian Heritage
By Dave Miller, Ph.D.

Interior design by Moisés Pinedo
Cover design by Rob Baker

Printed in China

Library of Congress Cataloging-in-Publication

Dave Miller (1953 -)
The Silencing of God: The Dismantling of America's Christian Heritage
Includes bibliographic references
ISBN: 978-1-60063-018-7
1. History of Christianity in North America. 2. Culture & institutions.
3. Systems of governments & states. 4. Constitutional & administrative law.
I. Title

277—dc22   2008933013

DEDICATION
To Deb—
whose positive influence on my
life has been inestimable,
profound, and eternal.

ACKNOWLEDGEMENT
Special thanks to Mike and Patsy Deasy—
dedicated servants of God.

CONTENTS

THE SILENCING
OF
GOD

DAVE MILLER, PH.D

FOR 185 YEARS, AMERICAN CULTURE WAS FRIENDLY TOWARD CHRISTIANITY. America was, in fact, considered a "Christian nation." After all, America has **never** been considered an Islamic, Buddhist, or Hindu nation, even as it has never been a **religionless** nation. But for the last 50 years, sinister forces—from humanism, atheism, and evolution, to social liberalism, pluralism, and "political correctness"—have been aggressive in their assault on the Christian religion. They have succeeded in gradually dismantling many of the moral and spiritual principles that once characterized society. America's religious, moral, and spiritual underpinnings are literally disintegrating.

Indeed, **America is at war!** This war is far more serious and deadly than any physical conflict (like the Iraq conflict). America is fighting a spiritual culture war. Regardless of the surface issues, **the central issue is—God.** Make no mistake: *America is in the throes of a life-and-death struggle over whether the God of the Bible will continue to be acknowledged as the one true God, and Christianity as the one true religion.*

Now more than ever before, social and political liberals—from Hollywood to the University to the nation's Capitol—are openly hostile toward God. Those who profess Christianity are facing the most perilous times ever faced in America. Every effort is being made to expunge references to God and Christianity from public life. Revisionist historians, liberal politicians, secularist educators, morally bankrupt entertainers, and activist judges, prodded by socialistic organizations like the ACLU (American Civil Liberties Union), AUSCS (Americans United for Separation of Church and State), PFAW (People for the American Way), NOW (National Organization for Women), Planned Parenthood, NARAL (National Abortion Rights Action League), and the NEA (National Educational Association), are feverishly reshaping our history, laws, and traditional way of life. [NOTE: The politically and socially liberal orientation of the NEA was demonstrated at its 2005 national convention with "its usual favoritism toward the gays and the feminists, hostility to parents, and support of liberal causes" (Schlafly, 2005).]

These sinister forces have mounted a massive, full-scale assault on traditional moral values. They are endeavoring to sanitize our society, cleansing it of its Christian connections. This conspiracy parades itself under the guise that the Founding Fathers and the *Constitution* advocated a "separation of church and state." The clever ploy goes something like this: "The Founders intended for our political institutions and public schools to be **religiously neutral**; a strict **church-state separation** must be observed, with religion completely excluded from the public sector; any such religious references would constitute an **illegal endorsement of religion by the government**." Thus, no references to God or Christianity in public settings must be allowed—whether in the government, the community, or the public school. This conspiratorial departure from the nation's origins, which has been spouted incessantly for some 50 years, has thoroughly permeated the American population and will surely go down in history as one of the big myths perpetrated on a people. For all practical purposes, America has become an atheistic, secularized, pluralistic state. Even the pagan monarchies of world history at least allowed their polytheistic beliefs to be incorporated into public life.

For the last half-century, in their orchestrated conspiracy to gain sanction for abortion, pornography, homosexuality, atheistic evolution, and a host of other evil, immoral behaviors and beliefs, "first amendment rights," "free speech," "intolerance!," and "censorship!" have been the whips that social liberals have used to beat, bull and berate their opponents into silent submission. But let on person utter even one peep of disagreement, and suddenl the "compassionate" liberals begin spewing **hate-speech** an hypocritically, **become completely intolerant, mean-spiri ed, and insensitive!**

Prior to the 1960s, when the Christian worldview tho oughly permeated American civilization, the anti-Christia forces demanded "equal time" and clamored for "freedom t express dissenting, alternative views." They derided the mo al majority by accusing them of using "Gestapo tactics" t suppress ideological opposition. But now that they, to a grea extent, have had their way, free speech and open discussio in the free market of ideas is out the window and opposin views are swiftly squelched. Talk about Gestapo tactics. Th anti-Christian forces in American society now exhibit th same intolerant mindset that has characterized totalitaria and communist regimes throughout history.

Undoubtedly, during the social ferment of the turbulen 1950s and 1960s, when subversive moral and religious ideol gies began to assert themselves, one of the strategic mistake made was permitting the instigators to redefine the histor cal terms and concepts as originally articulated by the arch tects of American civilization. "Free speech" was redefined t mean the right to practice and promote any and every ide or behavior that contradicted Christianity—no matter ho immoral or depraved. Everything from burning or urinating on the flag to hardcore pornography came to be classified as "free speech," while Christian resistance was considered "censorship." The minority within America who has exhibited hostility toward God, the Bible, and Christianity have lite ally intimidated and coerced the majority into accepting, a justification for their outrageous stance, the backing of the

Constitution. Yet, the historical evidence demonstrates that the Founders and Framers never would have countenanced the notion that "free speech" encompassed speech and behavior deemed "licentious," i.e., immoral, by Christian standards (see "Religion and the Founding...," 1998).

We live in a time warp far removed from America's origins. The Founders clearly believed that the initial existence and future survival of the Republic was heavily, if not exclusively, dependent on a perpetuated diffusion of the Bible and Christianity throughout society. Yet, for a half-century, Americans have been pounded and prodded with the propaganda that public expressions of Christianity should not be allowed lest we "offend" those who do not share our Christian beliefs. Who could have ever imagined that the day could come that the practice of the Christian religion in a Christian nation would be deemed "insensitive"?

To illustrate the extent to which America has plummeted from its original heights, while a Federal judge was demanding that the Chief Justice of the Alabama State Supreme Court remove a Ten Commandments monument in Montgomery, Alabama ("Chief Justice...," 2003), guess what was happening in California? A small marker was unveiled in Sacramento, California (Capitol Park) along the walkway of the California Veterans Memorial that reads: "In Honor of Gay, Lesbian, Bisexual, and Transgender Veterans Killed in Action" (Sanders, 2003). Gay-rights advocates hailed the memorial as

IN HONOR OF GAY, LESBIAN, BISEXUAL, AND TRANSGENDER VETERANS KILLED IN ACTION

Courtesy of Rich Hobson, The Foundation for Moral Law

the first such **state-sanctioned** landmark honoring homosexual war veterans.

Incredible! Honoring "gays" is praiseworthy, while honoring God is repugnant and "unconstitutional." This scenario is a microcosm of what is happening all over the nation. Allusions to the God of the Bible are being systematically stripped from public life—from Christian symbols in city and county seals, to pre-game prayers after school, to the use of the Bible in jury deliberation rooms (see Palm and Krannawitter, 2004; Hume, 2005; Johnson, 2005).

Never mind the fact that the phrase **"separation of church and state" is not even found in the** *Constitution*! (Thomas Jefferson used the term in a private letter to reassure Baptists that the government would not interfere in the free exercise of their religious beliefs [Jefferson, 1802].) In fact, labeling the phrase a "misguided analytical concept," and noting "the absence of a historical basis for this theory of rigid separation," the late U.S. Supreme Court Chief Justice William Rehnquist insightfully observed:

> It is impossible to build sound constitutional doctrine upon a mistaken understanding of constitutional history, but unfortunately the Establishment Clause has been expressly freighted with **Jefferson's misleading metaphor** for nearly 40 years.... The "wall of separation between church and State" is **a metaphor based on bad history**, a metaphor which has proved use-

less as a guide to judging. It should be **frankly and explicitly abandoned** (*Wallace v. Jaffree*, 472 U.S. 38[1985], 92,106-107, emp. added).

Is it true that the Founding Fathers and the *Constitution* intended for Christianity to be kept out of the public sector? Did they desire that references to God, Christ, and the Bible be excluded from public life? Or were they, in fact, actually more concerned with preventing the government from **interfering** with public expressions of the Christian religion? Did they, themselves, appeal frequently to God in political and public settings? Did they (and their descendants for the first 180+ years), in fact, recognize and subscribe to the critical principle: "Blessed is the nation whose God is the Lord" (Psalm 33:12)? Indeed, they did. I invite you to consider but a small portion of the massive amount of available evidence from the withered roots of America's forgotten and fast-fading heritage.

PUBLIC EXPRESSIONS OF GOD IN POLITICAL DOCUMENTS

THE DECLARATION

The *Declaration of Independence* is the premiere document that launched America as a new nation. Here is a quintessentially **political** document—a public expression of national concerns intended to articulate justification for declaring a separation from England. If the Founders intended to keep God out of national life, here was the perfect opportunity to manifest that intention. However, in this rela-

tively brief document, they used the following phrases: "Nature's God" (i.e., an 18th-century way to refer to the God Who created nature), "all men are **created** equal" and "endowed by their **Creator**," "appealing to the **Supreme Judge** of the world," and "with a firm reliance on the protection of **divine Providence**" (*The Declaration...*). Astounding! The 56 signers of the *Declaration of Independence*, in risking their very lives, put their signatures to a **political** document

Images courtesy of the National Archives and Records Administration that **acknowledged and appealed to the God of the Bible four times!** So much for their alleged insistence on "separation of church and state."

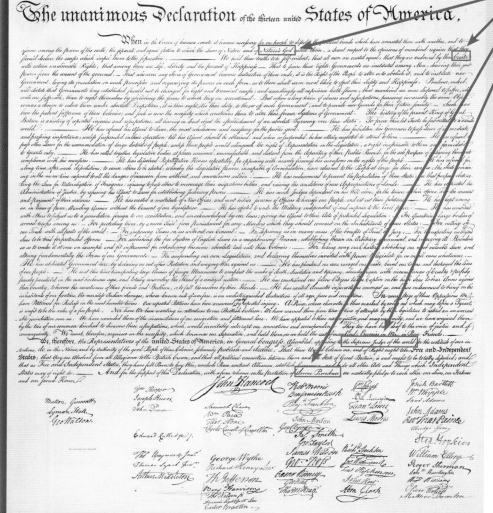

Courtesy of the National Archives and Records Administration

THE 56 FRAMERS OF THE DECLARATION OF INDEPENDENCE ACKNOWLEDGED THE GOD OF THE BIBLE!

THE FEDERAL CONSTITUTION

It is evident that the federal *Constitution* refrains from giving specific directives regarding Christianity. Why? The popular propaganda since the 1960s has been that "the irreligious Framers did not want the nation to retain any attachment to the Christian religion." Such an assertion is a monstrous perversion of historical fact. The truth of the matter is that they were fearful of the potential interference by the federal government in its ability to place restrictions on the free exercise of the Christian religion. Consequently, they desired that the specifics of religion be left up to the discretion of the several states. However, we must not think for a moment that the federal Framers did not sanction the nation's intimate affiliation with Christianity, or that they attempted to keep religion out of the *Constitution*. On the contrary, **the Christian religion is inherently assumed and implicitly present in the *Constitution*.**

In fact, the *United States Constitution* contains **a direct reference to Jesus Christ**! Consider three proofs for these contentions (*The United...*).

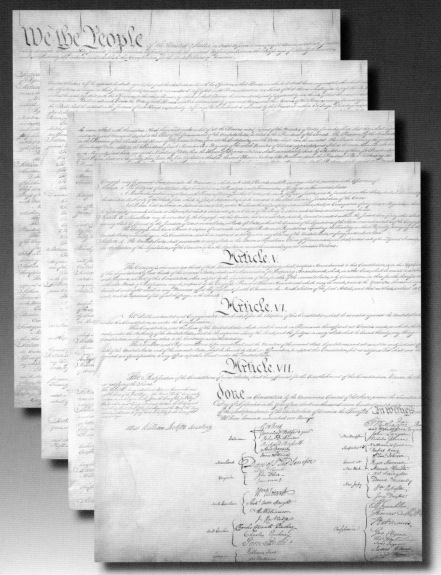

Images courtesy of the National Archives and Records Administration

First, consider the meaning of the First Amendment to the *Constitution*: "Congress shall make no law respecting an establishment of religion, or prohibiting the free exercise thereof...." We have been told that, by "establishment of religion," the Framers meant for the government to maintain complete religious neutrality and that pluralism ought to prevail, i.e., that all religions (whether Christianity, Islam, Buddhism, or Hinduism), though equally tolerated, must not be given any acknowledgement in the public sector. **But such an outlandish claim is absolutely false**. All one has to do is to go directly to the delegate discussions pertaining to the wording of the First Amendment in order to ascertain the context and original intent of the final wording (*Annals of Congress*, 1789, pp. 440ff.). The facts of the matter are that by their use of the term "religion," the Framers had in mind the several Protestant denominations. Their concern was to prevent any single Christian denomination from being elevated above the others and made the State religion—a circumstance that the Founders had endured under British rule when the Anglican Church was the state religion of the thirteen colonies. They further sought to leave the individual States free to make their own determinations with regard to religious (i.e., Christian) matters (cf. Story, 1833, 3.1873:730-731). The "Father of the

Bill of Rights," George Mason, actually proposed the following wording for the First Amendment, which demonstrates the context of their discussion regarding wording:

> [A]ll men have an equal, natural and unalienable right to the free exercise of religion, according to the dictates of conscience; and that **no particular sect or society of Christians** ought to be favored or established by law in preference to others (Rowland, 1892, 1:244, emp. added).

By "prohibiting the free exercise thereof," the Framers intended to convey that the federal government was not to interfere with the free and public practice of the **Christian** religion—the very thing that Christians are now experiencing.

Second, consider the wording of a sentence from Article I, Section 7 of the *Constitution*: "If any Bill shall not be returned by the President within ten Days (Sundays excepted) after it shall have been presented to him, the Same shall be a Law, in like Manner as if he had signed it...." **"Sundays excepted"**? So, the government shuts down and does not transact business on Sunday? Why? If this provision had been made in respect of Jews, the *Constitution* would have read "Saturdays excepted." If provision had been made for Muslims, the *Constitution* would have read "Fridays excepted." If the Founders

had intended to encourage a day of inactivity for the government without regard to any one religion, they could have chosen Monday, Tuesday, Wednesday, or Thursday. Instead, the federal *Constitution* reads "**Sundays** excepted"—proving conclusively that America was **Christian** in its orientation and that the Framers themselves shared the Christian worldview and gave **political recognition to and accommodation of that fact**.

Third, if these two allusions to Christianity are not enough, consider yet another. Immediately after Article VII, the *Constitution* closes with the following words:

> Done in Convention by the Unanimous Consent of the States present the Seventeenth Day of September in the Year of our Lord one thousand seven hundred and Eighty seven and of the Independence of the United States of America the Twelfth....

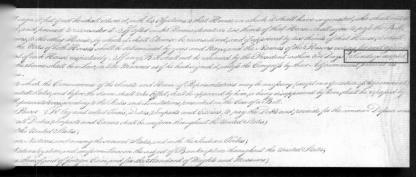

Did you catch it? Their work was done "in the Year of our Lord." The Christian world dates all of human history in terms of the birth of Christ. "B.C." means "before Christ," and "A.D." is the abbreviation for the Latin words "*anno Domini*," meaning "year of our Lord." If the Framers were interested in being pluralistic, multi-cultural, and politically correct, they would have refrained from using the B.C./A.D. designation. Or they would have used the religionless designations "C.E.," Common Era, and "B.C.E.," Before the Common Era (see "Common Era," 2008). In so doing, they would have avoided offending Jews, atheists, agnostics, and humanists. Or they could have used "A.H." (*anno hegirae*—which means "in the year of the Hijrah" and refers to Muhammad's flight from Mecca in A.D. 622), the date used by Muslims as the commencement date for the Islamic calendar. Instead, the Framers chose to utilize the dating method that indicated the worldview they shared. What's more, their reference to "our Lord" does not refer to a generic deity, nor does it refer even to God the Father. It refers to God the Son—**an explicit reference to Jesus Christ**. Make no mistake: the *Constitution of the United States* contains an explicit reference to Jesus Christ—not Allah, Buddha, Muhammad, nor the gods of Hindus or Native Americans! So, according to the thinking of the ACLU and a host of liberal educators, politicians, and judges, **the Constitution is—UNCONSTITUTIONAL**! Go figure.

ORIGINAL STATE CONSTITUTIONS

If the Framers wanted more direct references to Christianity to be left up to the several states, we would expect that the framers of state constitutions reflected that intention. And, indeed, they did. Once the Founders declared independence from England, each state commenced to hammer out their respective state constitutions, with the exception of Connecticut, which continued to operate under its "Fundamental Orders" until eventually formulating its own state constitution in 1818 (see Horton, 1988; Cohn, 1988). If one will take the time to examine the original state constitutions, one will be absolutely overwhelmed by the fact that those framers (many of whom were also involved in working on the federal *Constitution*), were intimately attached to the God of the Bible and deliberately reflected that attachment in their political pronouncements. The state constitution of the Commonwealth of Massachusetts, much the product of John Adams, provides just one sample. In "Part the First," the constitution reads:

> Article II. It is the right **as well as the duty** of all men in society, publicly, and at stated seasons **to worship the Supreme Being, the great Creator and Preserver of the universe**. And no subject shall be hurt, molested, or restrained, in his person, liberty, or estate, for **worshipping God** in the manner and season most agreeable to the dictates of his own conscience; or for his religious profession or sentiments; provided he doth not disturb the public peace, or obstruct others in their religious worship.

> Article III. As the happiness of a people, and the good order and preservation of civil government, essentially depend upon **piety, religion and morality**; and as these cannot be generally diffused through a community, but by the institution of **the public worship of God, and of public instructions in piety, religion and morality**: Therefore, to promote their happiness and to secure the good order and preservation of their government, the people of this commonwealth have a right to invest their legislature with power to authorize and require, and the legislature shall, from time to time, authorize and require, the several towns, parishes, precincts, and other bodies politic, or religious societies, **to make suitable provision, at their own expense, for the institution of the public worship of God, and for the support and**

maintenance of public Protestant teachers of piety, religion and morality**, in all cases where such provision shall not be made voluntarily (*Constitution of the Commonwealth...*, emp. added).

["Part the Second," the constitution enumerated the civil [power]s of the state:

Article I. There shall be a supreme executive magistrate, who shall be styled, The Governor of the Commonwealth of Massachusetts; and whose title shall be—His Excellency.

Article II. The governor shall be chosen [annually]; and no person shall be eligible to this office, unless at the time of his election, he shall have been an inhabitant of this commonwealth for seven years next preceding; and unless he shall at the same time, be seised in his own right, of a freehold within the commonwealth of the value of one thousand pounds; and **unless he shall declare himself to be of the Christian religion** (*Constitution of the Commonwealth...*, emp. added).

[Fur]ther, the "Oath of Office" that was to be taken by anyone [who] wished to serve as "governor, lieutenant governor, coun[cillor], senator or representative" began with the declaration: [I, A.B.], do declare, that **I believe the Christian religion, and [have] a firm persuasion of its truth**."

Massachusetts was typical. The average American would [be st]artled to know that of the original twelve state constitu[tions] (omitting Connecticut—whose founding documents [were a]lso riddled with references to God and Christianity; [*Fundamental Orders*, 1639; cf. *Fundamental Agreement...*, *Charter of Connecticut*, 1662), seven explicitly required [offic]e holders to be of the Protestant religion (i.e., Vermont, [New] Jersey, New Hampshire, Massachusetts, North Caro-

[Caro]lina, South Carolina, and Georgia). Maryland's constitution required a belief in the Christian religion. The constitutions of Delaware and Pennsylvania required a belief in the inspiration of the Old and New Testaments. While the Virginia and New York constitutions did not mandate an oath, they spoke of "Christian forbearance" and "no one denomination of Christians" above another ("State Constitutions," n.d.). When Connecticut finally wrote its own constitution, it, too, indicated the religion of the people to be Christianity (*Constitution of Connecticut*, 1818). **Observe: every single one of the original United States of America enacted constitutional acknowledgement of the one religion of Christianity.** Yet, incredibly, on the basis of current judicial interpretation, these original constitutions were—**UNCONSTITUTIONAL!**

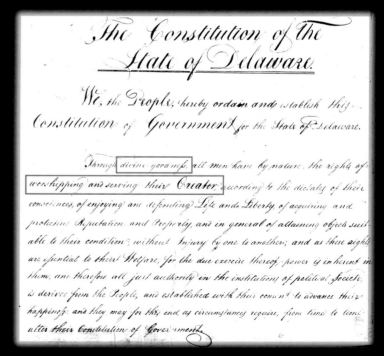

First page of the original, handwritten 1792 Delaware state constitution

CURRENT STATE CONSTITUTION PREAMBLES

Many more references to God and Christianity in governmental documents could be cited. In time, the state constitutions have gradually been amended to exclude such forthright religious allusions. Nevertheless, despite this erosion, of the present 50 state constitutions, 46 have "preambles." And **45 of those preambles make explicit, even passionate, appeals to the God of the Bible!** Here they are in alphabetical order (see "U.S. State...," 2003; emphasis is added in each):

ALABAMA

We, the people of the State of Alabama, in order to establish justice, insure domestic tranquility and secure the blessings of liberty to ourselves and our posterity, **invoking the favor and guidance of Almighty God**, do ordain and establish the following Constitution and form of government for the State of Alabama.

ALASKA

We the people of Alaska, **grateful to God** and to those who founded our nation and pioneered this great land, in order to secure and transmit to succeeding generations our heritage of political, civil, and **religious liberty** within the Union of States, do ordain and establish this constitution for the State of Alaska.

ARIZONA

We, the people of the State of Arizona, **grateful to Almighty God** for our liberties, do ordain this Constitution.

ARKANSAS

We, the people of the State of Arkansas, **grateful to Almighty God** for the privilege of choosing our own form of government, for our civil **and religious liberty**, and desiring to perpetuate its blessings and secure the same to our selves and posterity, do ordain and establish this Constitution.

CALIFORNIA

We, the People of the State of California, **grateful to Almighty God** for our freedom, in order to secure and perpetuate its blessings, do establish this Constitution.

COLORADO

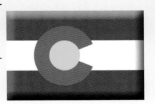

We the people of Colorado, **with profound reverence for the Supreme Ruler of the Universe**, in order to form a more independent and perfect government; establish justice; insure tranquility; provide for the common defense; promote the general welfare and secure the blessings of liberty to ourselves and our posterity, do ordain and establish this Constitution for the State of Colorado.

CONNECTICUT

The people of Connecticut **acknowledging with gratitude, the good providence of God**, in having permitted them to enjoy a free government, do, in order more effectually to define, secure, and perpetuate the liberties, rights and privileges which they have derived from their ancestors, hereby, after a careful consideration and revision, ordain and establish the following constitution and form of civil government.

DELAWARE

Through Divine goodness, all men have by nature the rights of worshipping and serving their Creator according to the dictates of their consciences, of enjoying and defending life and liberty, of acquiring and protecting reputation and property, and in general of obtaining objects suitable to their condition, without injury by one to another....

FLORIDA

We the people of the State of Florida, **being grateful to Almighty God** for our Constitutional liberty, in order to secure its benefits, do ordain and establish this Constitution.

GEORGIA

To perpetuate the principles of free government, insure justice to all, preserve peace, promote the interest and happiness of the citizen and of the family and transmit to posterity the enjoyment of liberty, we the people of Georgia, **relying upon the protection and guidance of Almighty God**, do ordain and establish this Constitution.

HAWAII

We, the people of Hawaii, **grateful for Divine Guidance**, and mindful of our Hawaiian heritage and uniqueness as an island State, dedicate our efforts to fulfill the philosophy decreed by the Hawaii State motto, "Ua mau ke ea o ka aina i ka pono"...do hereby ordain and establish this constitution for the State of Hawaii.

IDAHO

We the people of the State of Idaho, **grateful to Almighty God** for our freedom, to secure its blessings and promote our common welfare, do establish this Constitution.

ILLINOIS

We, the People of the State of Illinois—**grateful to Almighty God** for the civil, political and **religious liberty** which **He has permitted us to enjoy and seeking His blessing upon**

our endeavors—in order to provide for the health, safety and welfare of the people;...—do ordain and establish this Constitution for the State of Illinois.

INDIANA

We the people of the State of Indiana, **grateful to Almighty God** for the free exercise of the right to choose our own form of government, do ordain this Constitution.

IOWA

We the people of the State of Iowa, **grateful to the Supreme Being** for the blessings hitherto enjoyed, and **feeling our dependence on Him** for a continuation of those blessings, do ordain and establish a free and independent government, by the name of the State of Iowa....

KANSAS

We, the people of Kansas, **grateful to Almighty God** for our civil **and religious privileges**, in order to insure the full enjoyment of our rights as American citizens, do ordain and establish the Constitution of the State of Kansas, with the following boundaries, to wit....

KENTUCKY

We the people of the Commonwealth of Kentucky, **grateful to Almighty God** for the civil, political **and religious liberties** we enjoy, and invoking the continuance of these blessings, do ordain and establish this Constitution.

LOUISIANA

We, the people of Louisiana, **grateful to Almighty God** for the civil, political, economic, **and religious liberties** we enjoy, and desiring to protect individual rights to life, liberty, and property...do ordain and establish this constitution.

MAINE

We the people of Maine, in order to establish justice, insure tranquility, provide for our mutual defense, promote our common welfare, and secure to ourselves and our posterity the blessings of liberty, **acknowledging with grateful hearts the goodness of the Sovereign Ruler of the Universe** in affording us an opportunity, so favorable to the design; **and, imploring God's aid and direction** in its accomplishment...do ordain and establish the following Constitution for the government of the same.

MARYLAND

We, the People of the State of Maryland, **grateful to Almighty God** for our civil **and religious liberty**, and taking into our serious consideration the best means of establishing a good Constitution in this State for the sure foundation and more permanent security thereof, declare:

MASSACHUSETTS

...We, therefore, the people of Massachusetts, **acknowledging, with grateful hearts, the goodness of the great Legislator of the universe**, in affording us, **in the course of His providence**, an opportunity, deliberately and peaceably, without fraud, violence or surprise, of entering into an original, explicit, and solemn compact with each other; and of forming a new constitution of civil government, for ourselves and posterity; and **devoutly imploring His direction** in so interesting a design, do agree upon, ordain and establish the following *Declaration of Rights, and Frame of Government,* as the Constitution of the Commonwealth of Massachusetts.

MICHIGAN

We, the people of the State of Michigan, **grateful to Almighty God** for the blessings of freedom, and earnestly desiring to secure these blessings undiminished to ourselves and our posterity, do ordain and establish this constitution.

MINNESOTA

We, the people of the state of Minnesota, **grateful to God** for our civil **and religious liberty**, and desiring to perpetuate its blessings and secure the same to ourselves and our posterity, do ordain and establish this Constitution.

MISSISSIPPI

We, the people of Mississippi in convention assembled, **grateful to Almighty God, and involving his blessing on our work**, do ordain and establish this Constitution.

MISSOURI

We, the people of Missouri, **with profound reverence for the Supreme Ruler of the Universe, and grateful for His goodness**, do establish this Constitution for the better government of the State.

MONTANA

We the people of Montana **grateful to God** for the quiet beauty of our state, the grandeur of our mountains, the vastness of our rolling plains, and desiring to improve the quality of life, equality of opportunity and to secure the blessings of liberty for this and future generations do ordain and establish this constitution.

NEBRASKA

We, the people, **grateful to Almighty God** for our freedom, do ordain and establish the following declaration of rights and frame of government.

NEVADA

We the people of the State of Nevada, **grateful to Almighty God** for our freedom, in order to secure its blessings, insure domestic tranquility, and form a more perfect Government do establish this Constitution.

NEW JERSEY

We, the people of the State of New Jersey, **grateful to Almighty God** for the civil **and religious liberty which He hath so long permitted us to enjoy, and looking to Him for a blessing** upon our endeavors to secure and transmit the same unimpaired to succeeding generations, do ordain and establish this Constitution.

NEW MEXICO

We, the people of New Mexico, **grateful to Almighty God** for the blessings of liberty, in order to secure the advantages of a state government, do ordain and establish this Constitution.

NEW YORK

We the People of the State of New York, **grateful to Almighty God** for our Freedom, in order to secure its blessings, do establish this Constitution.

NORTH CAROLINA

We, the people of the State of North Carolina, **grateful to Almighty God, the Sovereign Ruler of Nations**, for the preservation of the American Union and the existence of our civil, political **and religious liberties**, and **acknowledging**  **our dependence upon Him for the continuance of those blessings** to us and our posterity, do, for the more certain security thereof and for the better government of this State, ordain and establish this Constitution.

NORTH DAKOTA

We, the people of North Dakota, **grateful to Almighty God** for the blessings of civil **and religious liberty**, do ordain and establish this constitution.

OHIO

We, the people of the State of Ohio, **grateful to Almighty God** for our freedom, to secure its blessings and promote our common welfare, do establish this Constitution.

OKLAHOMA

Invoking the guidance of Almighty God, in order to secure and perpetuate the blessing of liberty; to secure just and rightful government; to promote our mutual welfare and happiness, we, the people of the State of Oklahoma, do ordain and establish this Constitution.

PENNSYLVANIA

We, the people of the Commonwealth of Pennsylvania, **grateful to almighty God** for the blessings of civil **and religious liberty, and humbly invoking His guidance**, do ordain and establish this Constitution.

RHODE ISLAND

We, the people of the State of Rhode Island and Providence Plantations, **grateful to Almighty God** for the civil **and religious liberty which He hath so long permitted us to enjoy, and looking to Him for a blessing upon our endeavors** to secure and to transmit the same, unimpaired, to succeeding generations, do ordain and establish this Constitution of government.

SOUTH CAROLINA

We, the people of the State of South Carolina, in Convention assembled, **grateful to God** for our liberties, do ordain and establish this Constitution for the preservation and perpetuation of the same.

SOUTH DAKOTA

We, the people of South Dakota, **grateful to Almighty God** for our civil **and religious liberties**, in order to form a more perfect and independent government... do ordain and establish this constitution for the state of South Dakota.

TEXAS

Humbly invoking the blessings of Almighty God, the people of the State of Texas, do ordain and establish this Constitution.

UTAH

Grateful to Almighty God for life and liberty, we, the people of Utah, in order to secure and perpetuate the principles of free government, do ordain and establish this Constitution.

WASHINGTON

We, the people of the State of Washington, **grateful to the Supreme Ruler of the Universe** for our liberties, do ordain this constitution.

WEST VIRGINIA

We the people of West Virginia, **through Divine Providence**, enjoy the blessings of liberty and **reaffirm our faith in and constant reliance upon God.**

WISCONSIN

We, the people of Wisconsin, **grateful to Almighty God** for our freedom, in order to secure its blessings...do establish this Constitution.

WYOMING

We, the people of the State of Wyoming, **grateful to God** for our civil, political **and religious liberties**, and desiring to secure them to ourselves and perpetuate them to our posterity, do ordain and establish this Constitution.

Of the 46 state constitutions that contain Preambles, only Oregon has no reference to God. Hence, 45 of the 50 state constitutions refer to the God of the Bible. The objective observer is forced to conclude that the original framers of the state constitutions shared the same belief in and reliance on the same God that the national Framers possessed. If the notion of "separation of church and state" were correct, why did the framers of the state constitutions unashamedly include such glaring, forthright acknowledgements of God? And why have those allusions remained to this day? On the basis of today's ludicrous, inane standard, **45 of the state constitutions are, and have always been—UNCONSTITUTIONAL.**

PRESIDENTIAL INAUGURAL ADDRESSES

Immediately after taking the oath of office, Presidents of the United States deliver to the nation an inaugural address. Few people are probably aware of the fact that, in doing so, **every single President of the United States has alluded to the God of the Bible!** The further back in history, the more extensive the allusions to God. For example, on Thursday, April 30, 1789, the first President of our country, George Washington, made the following remarks:

Such being the impressions under which I have, in obedience to the public summons, repaired to the present station, it would be peculiarly improper to omit in this first official act my fervent supplications to **that Almighty Being who rules over the universe, who presides in the councils of nations, and whose providential aids can supply every human defect**, that **His** benediction may consecrate to the liberties and happiness of the people of the United States a Government instituted by themselves for these essential purposes, and may enable every instrument employed in its administration to execute with success the functions allotted to his charge. In tender-

George Washington

ing this homage to **the Great Author of every public and private good**, I assure myself that it expresses your sentiments not less than my own, nor those of my fellow-citizens at large less than either. No people can be bound to acknowledge and adore **the Invisible Hand which conducts the affairs of men** more than those of the United States. Every step by which they have advanced to the character of an independent nation seems to have been distinguished by some token of **providential agency**; since we ought to be no less persuaded that **the propitious smiles of Heaven** can never be expected on a nation that disregards **the eternal rules of order and right which Heaven itself has ordained**.... Having thus imparted to you my sentiments as they have been awakened by the occasion which brings us together, I shall take my present leave; but not without resorting once more to **the benign Parent of the Human Race** in humble supplication that, since **He** has been pleased to favor the American people with opportunities for deliberating in perfect tranquility,...so **His divine blessing** may be equally conspicuous in the enlarged views, the temperate consultations, and the wise measures on which the success of this Government must depend (1789, emp. added).

Such remarks not only reflect a deep sense of dependency on and intimacy with the God of the Bible, they demonstrate the extent to which **the entire nation** integrated this conviction into national, public life.

The second President of the United States, John Adams, made the following remarks in his inaugural speech on Sat-

John Adams

Relying, however, on the purity of their intentions, the justice of their cause, and the integrity and intelligence of the people, **under an overruling Providence which had so signally protected this country from the first**, the representatives of this nation, then consisting of little more than half its present number, not only broke to pieces the chains which were forging and the rod of iron that was lifted up, but frankly cut asunder the ties which had bound them, and launched into an ocean of uncertainty.... And **may that Being who is supreme over all, the Patron of Order, the Fountain of Justice, and the Protector in all ages of the world of virtuous liberty**, continue **His blessing** upon this nation and its Government and give it all possible success and duration consistent with the ends of **His providence** (1797, emp. added).

Thomas Jefferson's first inaugural on March 4, 1801 included the following words:

...acknowledging and adoring **an overruling Providence**, which by all its dispensations proves that it delights in the happiness of man here and his greater happiness hereafter—with all these blessings, what more is necessary to make us a happy and a prosperous people?.... And may **that Infinite Power which rules the destinies of the universe** lead our councils to what is best, and give them a favorable issue for your peace and prosperity (1801

Thomas Jefferson

In his second inaugural address on March 4, 1805, Jefferson announced:

> ...I shall need, too, the favor of **that Being in whose hands we are**, who led our forefathers, as Israel of old, from their native land, and planted them in a country flowing with all the necessaries and comforts of life; who has covered our infancy with **his providence**, and our riper years with **his wisdom and power**; and to whose goodness I ask you to **join with me in supplications, that he will so enlighten the minds of your servants, guide their councils, and prosper their measures**, that whatsoever they do, shall result in your good, and shall secure to you the peace, friendship, and approbation of all nations (1805, emp. added).

Such remarks by one of the least religious of the Founders hardly sounds like the anti-Christian "deist" that he has been represented to be. He believed in the God of the Bible—the same One Who had guided the Israelites as reported in the Old Testament—and believed that He had guided the founding of America and was **actively influencing** America and her leaders.

Moving along in American history, on March 4, 1841, William Henry Harrison's inaugural address included these astounding remarks:

> I deem the present occasion sufficiently important and solemn to justify me in expressing to my fellow-citizens **a profound reverence for the Christian religion** and a thorough conviction that **sound morals, religious liberty, and a just sense of religious responsibility** are essentially connected with

all true and lasting happiness; and to **that good Being who has blessed us** by the gifts of civil and religious freedom, **who watched over and prospered** the labors of our fathers and **has hitherto preserved to us** institutions far exceeding in excellence those of any other people, let us unite in fervently commending every interest of our beloved country in all future time (1841, emp. added).

Like his presidential predecessors, not to mention the Founders themselves, here was a President who would be deemed by today's standards to be wholly and unequivocally politically incorrect. Observe carefully his forthright contentions: (1) being inaugurated as President of the United States is sufficiently significant to express to the entire nation and the world profound respect for **Christianity**—not Islam, Buddhism, Hinduism, Judaism, or atheism; (2) all true and lasting happiness **depend** on Christian morality, freedom to practice Christianity, and a proper/just sense of **religious** (not social or political) responsibility; (3) the civil and religious freedom enjoyed by Americans **came from God**; (4) America's political institutions are **superior** to all other countries; and (5) America's future **is dependant on God**. Illegal endorsement of religion by government? Ridiculous!

On Monday, March 4, 1861, when Abraham Lincoln became President, the nation was standing on the brink of imminent civil war. If you had been in that crucial position on that momentous occasion, what would you have said? In his inaugural address, it is evident that the God of the Bible and the Christian religion weighed heavily on his mind:

> My countrymen, one and all, think calmly and well upon this whole

subject. Nothing valuable can be lost by taking time. If there be an object to hurry any of you in hot haste to a step which you would never take deliberately, that object will be frustrated by taking time; but no good object can be frustrated by it. Such of you as are now dissatisfied still have the old Constitution unimpaired, and, on the sensitive point, the laws of your own framing under it;... If it were admitted that you who are dissatisfied hold the right side in the dispute, there still is no single good reason for precipitate action. Intelligence, patriotism, **Christianity, and a firm reliance on Him who has never yet forsaken this favored land** are still competent to adjust in the best way all our present difficulty (1861, emp. added).

Imagine that! Abraham Lincoln used as the central rational to avert the War Between the States the fact that they all shared the same God and the same religion!

Moving into the 20th century, on March 4, 1921, fresh out of World War I, Warren G. Harding delivered his inaugural speech:

> One cannot stand in this presence and be unmindful of the tremendous responsibility. The world upheaval has added heavily to our tasks. But with the realization comes the surge of high resolve, and there is reassurance in belief in **the God-given destiny of our Republic**. If I felt that there is to be sole responsibility in the Executive for the America of tomorrow I should shrink from the burden. But here are a hundred millions, with common concern and shared responsibility, **answerable to God** and country. The Republic summons them to their duty, and I invite co-operation. I accept my part with single-mindedness of purpose and humility of spirit, and implore **the favor and guidance of God in His Heaven**. With these I am unafraid, and confidently face the future. I have taken the solemn oath of office on that **passage of Holy Writ** wherein it is asked: "**What doth the Lord require of thee but to do justly, and to love mercy, and to walk humbly with thy God?**" [Micah 6:8—DM]. This I plight **to God** and country (1921, emp. added).

Who was viewed as directing the destiny of America? God! To whom was the president answerable? To God! To Whom did he appeal for guidance? To God! On what object did he take the oath of office? The Word of God! To Whom did he "plight" (i.e., solemnly pledge) himself? To God! Such words certainly conflict with the current alleged restriction between church and state.

Four years later, on Wednesday, March 4, 1925, Calvin Coolidge commenced his presidency with the following words:

> Here stands our country, an example of tranquility at home, a patron of tranquility abroad. Here stands its Government, **aware of its might but obedient to its conscience**. Here it will continue to stand, seeking peace and prosperity,...attentive to the intuitive counsel of womanhood, encouraging education, desiring **the advancement of religion**, supporting the cause of justice and honor among the nations. America seeks no earthly empire built on blood and force. No ambition, no temptation, lures her to thought of foreign dominions. The legions which she sends forth are armed, not with the sword, but with **the cross**. The higher state

to which she seeks the allegiance of all mankind is not of human, but of **divine origin. She cherishes no purpose save to merit the favor of Almighty God** (1925, emp. added).

This President claimed that America may not be justly styled an aggressor nation—since the nation embraces Christianity. Indeed, he insisted that America's **only purpose** is to please God and to urge all nations to do the same by giving their allegiance to Him.

This examination of presidential inaugural addresses could be greatly expanded. Do not miss the point: In direct contradiction to the attempt to expel God from the government and public life, so far **every single President of the United States has referred to the God of the Bible at one or more of his inaugurations.**

PRESIDENTIAL OATH
OF OFFICE

Article II, Section 1 of the *Constitution of the United States* gives the precise wording of the oath of office to be taken by every individual who is elected to the presidency ("Presidential Oaths..."). Conspicuously absent from the oath are the closing words so familiar to our ears: "So help me God." When did these final four words that affirm belief in the God of the Bible begin to be added to the presidential oath of office? The custom began on April 30, 1789 when **the very first President** sworn into office, George Washington, took it upon himself to add the words. **Every President thereafter** has followed Washington's lead by adding the words "so help me God" (Yoffe, 2000). The oath mandated for the Vice President (and all other government employees), which is set out

in the *U.S. Code*, actually mandates the phrase "so help me God" (2002, 5USC3331). What's more, history records that after taking the oath, George Washington then leaned down and **kissed the Bible** ("President George...," n.d.)! That tradition was followed by his successors until Benjamin Pierce broke the precedent in 1853, yet all have continued the traditions of placing their hand on **the Bible** and repeating "so help me God" at the conclusion of the oath ("Inaugurals of Presidents..."). Unconstitutional? Separation of church and state? Absurd!

PRESIDENTIAL SPEECHES

On Monday, December 8, 1941, before a joint session of Congress, the President of the United States, Franklin Delano Roosevelt, delivered a historic speech in which he urged Congress to issue a formal declaration of war against Japan. In that speech, he openly declared the national attitude regarding God's role in the impending struggle:

To the Congress of the United States: Yesterday, December 7, 1941—a date which will live in infamy—the United States of America was suddenly and deliberately

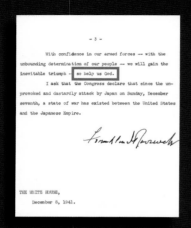

attacked by naval and air forces of the Empire of Japan…. The attack yesterday on the Hawaiian Islands has caused severe damage to American naval and military forces. Very many American lives have been lost…. No matter how long it may take us to overcome this premeditated invasion, the American people, in their righteous might, will win through to absolute victory. I believe I interpret the will of the Congress and of the people when I assert that we will not only defend ourselves to the uttermost but will make very certain that this form of treachery shall never endanger us again. Hostilities exist. There is no blinking at the fact that our people, our territory, and our interests are in grave danger. With confidence in our armed forces—with the unbounded determination of our people—we will gain the inevitable triumph—**so help us God**. I ask that the Congress declare that since the unprovoked and dastardly attack by Japan on Sunday, December 7, a state of war has existed between the United States and the Japanese Empire (Roosevelt, 1941, emp. added).

On May 6, 1982, Ronald Reagan delivered the following remarks at a White House ceremony in observance of the National Day of Prayer—words that resemble the Founders' own frequent admonitions:

[A]ll of us are here with a common purpose: to observe on National Day of Prayer, a tradition that was begun by the Continental Congress—that the first Thursday of May would be such a day. Prayer has sustained our people in crisis, strengthened us in times of challenge, and guided us through our daily lives since the first settlers came to this continent. Our forebearers came not for gold, but mainly **in search of God** and the freedom to worship in their own way. We've been a free people living under the law, with **faith in our Maker** and in our future. I've said before that the most sublime picture in American history is of George Washington on his knees in the snow at Valley Forge. That image personifies a people who know that it's not enough to depend on our own courage and goodness; **we must also seek help from God, our Father and Preserver**…. Today, prayer is still a powerful force in America, and **our faith in God is a mighty source of strength**. Our Pledge of Allegiance states that we are "one nation under God," and our currency bears the motto, "In God We Trust." The morality and values such faith implies are deeply embedded in our national character. Our country embraces those principles by design, and we abandon them at our peril. Yet in recent years, well-meaning Americans in the name of freedom have taken freedom away. For the sake of religious tolerance, they've forbidden religious practice in our public classrooms. The law of this land has effectively removed prayer from our

Top left: Third page of FDR's speech to Congress on December 8, 1941. Top right: FDR signing the Declaration of War against Japan, December 8, 1941. Bottom: The USS Arizona burning after the Japanese attack on Pearl Harbor, December 7, 1941. Courtesy of the National Archives and Records Administration

classrooms. **How can we hope to retain our freedom through the generations if we fail to teach our young that our liberty springs from an abiding faith in our Creator?** Thomas Jefferson once said, "Almighty God created the mind free." But current interpretation of our Constitution holds that the minds of our children cannot be free to pray to God in public schools. No one will ever convince me that a moment of voluntary prayer will harm a child or threaten a school or State. But I think it can strengthen our faith in **a Creator who alone has the power to bless America**.... I have never believed that the oft-quoted [first] amendment was supposed to protect us from religion. **It was to protect religion from government tyranny**. Together, let us take up the challenge to reawaken America's religious and moral heart, recognizing that a deep and abiding **faith in God is the rock upon which this great Nation was founded** (1982, emp. added).

SPEECHES AND QUOTES BY FOUNDERS

As one peruses the plethora of speeches, writings, and private correspondence left behind by the Founders, he is literally overwhelmed by their incessant allusion to the critical importance of God and Christianity to national life. One of the great Founders of America was Patrick Henry. On March 23, 1775, over a year before the *Declaration of Independence*, he attended the Second Virginia Convention (which, by the way, met in a church building in Richmond) to discuss the tyranny of the Crown. The 39-year-old delegate from Hanover County took a seat on the third pew, patiently listening to the pleas of the Tories to refrain from antagonizing the King of England by further talk of independence. When his

Patrick Henry

opportunity to speak finally came, he rose and delivered the following spectacular speech—a speech that cannot be used in the public school system of America today because of its frequent, now deemed politically incorrect, allusion to God and the Bible. [NOTE: Lest the reader miss the fact that Henry's speech is thoroughly saturated with references to God and the Bible, such allusions are noted in bold and direct biblical citations are italicized and bracketed]:

No man thinks more highly than I do of the patriotism, as well as abilities, of the very worthy gentlemen who have just addressed the House. But different men often see the same subject in different lights; and, therefore, I hope it will not be thought disrespectful to those gentlemen if, entertaining as I do opinions of a character very opposite to theirs, I shall speak forth my sentiments freely and without reserve. This is no time for ceremony. The question before the House is one of awful moment to this country. For my own part, I consider it as nothing less than a question of freedom or slavery; and in proportion to the magnitude of the subject ought to be the freedom of the debate. It is only in this way that we can hope to arrive at truth, and fulfill **the great responsibility which we hold to God** and our country. Should I keep back my opinions at such a time, through fear of giving offense, I should consider myself as guilty of treason towards my country, and of an act of disloyalty toward **the Majesty of Heaven, which I revere above all earthly kings**.

Mr. President, it is natural to man to indulge in the illusions of hope. We are apt to shut our eyes against a painful truth, and listen to the song of that siren till she transforms us into beasts. Is this the part of wise men, engaged in a great and arduous struggle for liberty? Are we disposed to be of the number of those who, **having eyes, see not, and, having ears, hear not,** [*Mark 8:18*] the things which so nearly concern their temporal salvation? For my part, whatever anguish of spirit it may cost, I am willing to know the whole truth; to know the worst, and to provide for it. I have but one lamp by which my feet are guided, and that is the lamp of experience. I know of no way of judging of the future but by the past. And judging by the past, I wish to know what there has been in the conduct of the British ministry for the last ten years to justify those hopes with which gentlemen have been pleased to **solace themselves** [*Proverbs 7:18*] and the House. Is it that insidious smile with which our petition has been lately received? Trust it not, sir; it will prove **a snare to your feet** [*Jeremiah 18:22*]. Suffer not yourselves to be **betrayed with a kiss** [*Luke 22:48*]. Ask yourselves how this gracious reception of our petition comports with those warlike preparations which cover our waters and darken our land. Are fleets and armies necessary to a work of love and reconciliation? Have we shown ourselves so unwilling to be reconciled that force must be called in to win back our love? Let us not **deceive ourselves** [*James 1:22; 1 John 1:8*], sir. These are the implements of war and subjugation; the last arguments to which kings resort…. I ask gentlemen, sir, what means this martial array, if its purpose be not to force us to submission? Can gentlemen assign any other possible motive for it? Has Great Britain any enemy, in this quarter of the world, to call for all this accumulation of navies and armies? No, sir, she has none. They are meant for us: they can be meant for no other. They are sent over to bind and rivet upon us those chains which the British ministry have been so long forging. And what have we to oppose to them? Shall we try argument? Sir, we have

Patrick Henry

been trying that for the last ten years. Have we anything new to offer upon the subject? Nothing. We have held the subject up in every light of which it is capable; but it has been all in vain. Shall we resort to entreaty and humble supplication? What terms shall we find which have not been already exhausted? Let us not, I beseech you, sir, **deceive ourselves** [*James 1:22; 1 John 1:8*]. Sir, we have done everything that could be done to avert the storm which is now coming on. We have petitioned; we have remonstrated; we have supplicated; we have prostrated ourselves before the throne, and have implored its interposition to arrest the tyrannical hands of the ministry and Parliament. Our petitions have been slighted; our remonstrances have produced additional violence and insult; our supplications have been disregarded; and we have been spurned, with contempt, from the foot of the throne! In vain, after these things, may we indulge the fond hope of peace and reconciliation. There is no longer any room for hope. If we wish to be free—if we mean to preserve inviolate those inestimable privileges for which we have been so long contending—if we mean not basely to abandon the noble struggle in which we have been so long engaged, and which we have pledged ourselves never to abandon until the glorious object of our contest shall be obtained—we must fight! I repeat it, sir, we must fight! An appeal to arms and to **the God of hosts** [*term used 40 times in the Old Testament for God in His military might—DM*] is all that is left us!

They tell us, sir, that we are weak; unable to cope with so formidable an adversary. But when shall we be stronger? Will it be the next week, or the next year? Will it be when we are totally disarmed, and when a British guard shall be stationed in every house? Shall we gather strength by irresolution and inaction? Shall we acquire the means of effectual resistance by lying supinely on our backs and hugging the delusive phantom of hope, until our enemies shall have **bound us hand and foot**? [*Matthew 22:13*] Sir, we are not weak if we make a proper use of those means which **the God of nature** hath placed in our power. Three millions of people, armed in the holy cause of liberty, and in such a country as that which we possess, are invincible by any force which our enemy can send against us. Besides, sir, we shall not fight our battles alone. **There is a just God who presides over the destinies of nations**, and who will raise up friends **to fight our battles for us** [*2 Chronicles 32:8*]. **The battle, sir, is not to the strong alone** [*Ecclesiastes 9:11*]; it is to the vigilant, the active, the brave. Besides, sir, we have no election. If we were base enough to desire it, it is now too late to retire from the contest. There is no retreat but in submission and slavery! Our chains are forged! Their clanking may be heard on the plains of Boston! The war is inevitable—and let it come! I repeat it, sir, let it come.

It is in vain, sir, to extenuate the matter. Gentlemen may cry, **Peace, Peace—but there is no peace** [*Jeremiah 6:14*]. The war is actually begun! The next gale that sweeps from the north will bring to our ears the clash of resounding arms! Our brethren are already in the field! **Why stand we here idle?** [*Matthew 20:6*] What is it that gentlemen wish? What would they have? Is life so dear, or peace so sweet, as to be purchased at the price of chains and slavery? Forbid it, **Almighty God**! I know not what course others may take; but as for me, give me liberty or give me death! (1775, emp., italics, and bracketed material added).

Patrick Henry's frequent appeals to God were typical of the Founders. They assigned a **theological** rationale for the Revolutionary War. They viewed the effort to achieve independent national existence as sanctioned by and dependent on the God of the Bible. Such facts have been all but expunged from American history courses. Indeed, how many American history teachers today even recognize the multiplicity of Bible quotations in Henry's famous speech?

After independence was achieved, the Founders met for the purpose of hammering out the political principles that would guide the new nation. On June 28, 1787, in the Constitutional Convention in Philadelphia, one of the least religious of the Founders, Benjamin Franklin, now in his 80s, rose to his feet and made the following majestic remarks [NOTE: Allusions to God and the Bible are noted in bold and direct biblical citations are italicized and bracketed]:

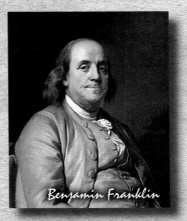

Benjamin Franklin

In this situation of this Assembly, groping as it were in the dark to find political truth, and scarce able to distinguish it when presented to us, how has it happened, Sir, that we have not hitherto once thought of humbly applying to **the Father of lights** [*James 1:17*], to illuminate our understanding? In the beginning of the contest with Britain, when we were sensible of danger, **we had daily prayer in this room for divine protection**. Our prayers, Sir, were heard and they were graciously answered. And have we now forgotten **that powerful friend**? Or, do we imagine we no longer need **his assistance**? I have lived, Sir, a long time, and the longer I live, the more **convincing proofs** [*Acts 1:3*] I see of this truth—that **God governs in the affairs of men** [*Daniel 4:17*]. And if **a sparrow cannot fall to the ground without his notice** [*Matthew 10:29*], is it probable that an empire can rise without his aid?

We have been assured, Sir, in the **Sacred Writings**, that "**except the Lord build the House, they labor in vain that build it**" [*Psalm 127:1*]. I firmly believe this; and I also believe that without **his concurring aid** we shall succeed in this political building no better than the **Builders of Babel** [*Genesis 11*]: We shall be divided by our partial local interests; our projects will be confounded, and we ourselves shall become **a reproach and bye word down to future ages** [*Psalm 44:13-14; Jeremiah 24:9*]. I therefore beg leave to move—that henceforth **prayers imploring the assistance of Heaven, and its blessing** on our deliberations, be held in this Assembly every morning before we proceed to business, and that one or more of the clergy of this city be requested to officiate in that service (1787, emp., italics, and bracketed material added).

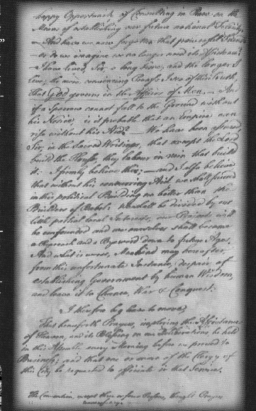

These two speeches by Patrick Henry and Benjamin Franklin would now be deemed politically incorrect and inappropriate for public schools (unless significantly "abridged"). Even if they were admitted to the history classroom, how many of today's American history teachers, let alone students, would even recognize the multiple quotations from the Bible?

After serving as the Commander-in-Chief of the American revolutionary military forces, and then serving two terms as the nation's first president, George Washington delivered his farewell address to the nation before retiring to private life. In that speech, he pinpointed the critical foundation for the survival of the nation:

Of all the dispositions and habits which lead to political prosperity, **religion and morality** are indispensable supports. In vain would that man claim the tribute of patriotism, who should labor to subvert these great pillars of human happiness, these firmest props of the duties of men and citizens. The mere politician, equally with the pious man, ought to respect and to cherish them. A volume could not trace all their connections with private and public felicity. Let it simply be asked: Where is the security for property, for reputation, for life, if the sense of **religious obligation** desert the oaths which are the instruments of investigation in courts of justice? And let us with caution indulge the supposition that **morality** can be maintained **without religion**. Whatever may be conceded to the influence of refined education on minds of

Top: Benjamin Franklin's speech to the Constitutional Convention, June 28, 1787. Courtesy of the Library of Congress
Bottom: Senate Chaplain Zebarney Phillips opens the Senate session with a prayer, February 21, 1939. Courtesy of the U.S. Senate Historical Office

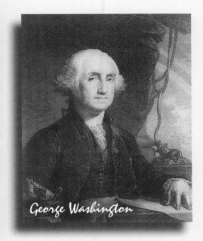
George Washington

peculiar structure, **reason and experience both forbid us to expect that national morality can prevail in exclusion of religious principle.** It is substantially true that **virtue or morality is a necessary spring of popular government**. The rule, indeed, extends with more or less force to every species of free government. Who that is a sincere friend to it can look with indifference upon attempts to shake the foundation of the fabric? (1796, emp. added).

The first President of the United States—the Father of our country—declared that religion and morality are absolutely indispensable to the perpetuation of "political prosperity," "human happiness," and "popular government"! He insisted that the morality of the citizens of the nation cannot be main-

tained without the Christian religion. He further affirmed that anyone who attempts to undermine the religious foundation of the country is lacking in patriotism and is no friend to the Republic.

The sixth President of the United States, John Quincy Adams, reflecting on the origin of the nation, stated succinctly the role that God played in America's founding:

> From the day of the Declaration, the people of the North American Union and of its constituent states were associated bodies of civilized men and **Christians**.... They were bound by **the laws of God, which they all**, and by **the laws of the Gospel**, which they **nearly** all, acknowledged as the rules of their conduct (1821, p. 28, emp. added).

John Quincy Adams

The Declaration of Independence cast off all the shackles of this [British] dependency. The United States of America were no longer Colonies. They were **an independent nation of Christians** (1837, p. 18, emp. added).

Observe carefully that President Adams claimed that all of the Founders believed in the God of the Bible, and that nearly all of them also believed in Christianity. Since John Quincy Adam's father was a prominent Founder as well as the second President of the United States, surely he was in a much better position to assess America's founding principles and the intentions of the Founders than anyone today. Yet, the public school system of America since the 1960s has been perpetrating on unsuspecting children the outrageous falsehood

George Washington's Farewell Address, 1796. Courtesy of the Library of Congress that the Founders did not express allegiance to the Christian religion, but were deists at most and more generally irreligious. Who is more qualified to make such an assessment: anti-American, anti-Christian, biased, revisionist historians/educators from the last 50 years—or John Quincy Adams?

Noah Webster, known for his tireless efforts to standardize American English, had much to say about the spiritual underpinnings of America's government:

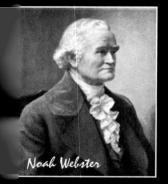

Noah Webster

> In my view, the **Christian religion is the most important and one of the first things** in which all children, under a free government, ought to be instructed.... No truth is more evident to my mind than that the **Christian religion must be the basis of any government** intended to secure the rights and privileges of a free people (1843, p. 291, emp. added).
>
> The **Christian religion**, in its purity, is the basis, or rather **the source of all genuine freedom in government**.... and I am persuaded that **no civil government of a republican form can exist and be durable** in which the principles of **that** religion have not a controlling influence (Snyder, 1990, p. 253, emp. added).

Again, Webster's remarks are very typical of the Founders in their adamant and repetitious insistence that our form of government can neither be sustained nor perpetuated without the widespread diffusion of Christian principles throughout society.

In a speech to the First Provincial Congress of New Jersey on November 4, 1782, Elias Boudinot, who became President of the Continental Congress, admonished his fellows:

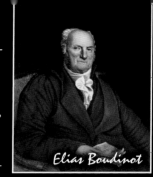

Elias Boudinot

> Let us enter on this important [duty]... under the idea that **we are Christians** on whom the eyes of the world are now turned.... **Let us earnestly call and beseech him for Christ's sake to preside in our councils** (1896, 1:19, emp. added).

Question: In making such a statement, did President Boudinot say anything that would have been instantly decried as a "violation of church and state" or an insensitive attempt to press his religious beliefs on others? Quite the opposite. The fact that history records this admonition is proof that he was merely expressing the sentiments of the bulk of his contemporaries.

In what today would be deemed thoroughly politically incorrect, George Washington explained in a speech to the Delaware Indian chiefs in 1779: "You do well to wish to learn our arts and ways of life, and above all, **the religion of Jesus Christ**. These will make you a greater and happier people than you are. Congress will do everything they can to assist you in this wise intention" (1932, 15:55, emp. added).

Several volumes could be written documenting the forthright expressions made by the majority of the Founders indicating their commitment to the Christian religion. Consider the following scattered quotations from but a few of the signers of the *Declaration* and the *Constitution* in which their preference for the Christian religion is self-evident. *Declaration* signer, John Witherspoon, declared that "the **Christian** religion is superior to

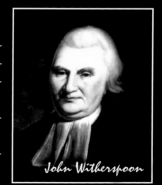

John Witherspoon

Charles Carroll

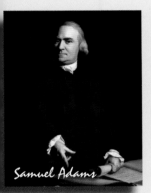

Samuel Adams

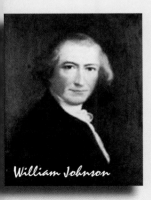

William Johnson

every other…. [T]here is not only an excellence in the **Christian** morals, but a manifest superiority in them to those which are derived from any other source" (1815, 8:33,38). In a letter to James McHenry on November 4, 1800, *Declaration* signer, Charles Carroll, observed: "[W]ithout morals a republic cannot subsist any length of time; they therefore who are decrying **the Christian religion**…are undermining the solid foundation of morals, the best security for the duration of free governments" (as quoted in Steiner, 1907, p. 475, emp. added). *Declaration* signer Samuel Adams called on citizens to educate their children in "the study and practice of the exalted virtues of **the Christian system**" (Adams and Adams, 1802, p. 10, emp. added). *Declaration* signer William Ellery, in speaking of the continued "growth of Christian knowledge," asserted: "The attempt to **Christianize** the heathen world and to produce peace on earth and goodwill towards men is humane, **Christian**, and sublime" (as quoted in Sparks, 1860, 6:139, emp. added).

Constitution signer, William Johnson, admonished: "Your first great duties, you are sensible, are those you owe **to Heaven, to your Creator and Redeemer**. Let these be ever present to your minds, and exemplified in your lives and conduct…. [L]et us take

Gunning Bedford

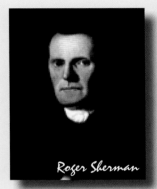

Roger Sherman

Alexander Hamilton

William Ellery

care that our **Christianity**, though put to the test…be not shaken, and that our love for things really good wax not cold" (as quoted in Beardsley, 1886, pp. 142,184, emp. added). *Constitution* signer, Jacob Broom, urged his son in 1794: "[D]on't forget to be a **Christian**. I have said much to you on this head and I hope an indelible impression is made" (see Barton, 2002, p. 137, emp. added). *Constitution* signer, Gunning Bedford, declared in a funeral oration: "Now to the triune **God, the Father, the Son, and the Holy Ghost**, be ascribed all honor and dominion, forevermore—Amen" (1800, p. 18). Roger Sherman, signer of both the *Constitution* and the *Declaration*, expressed his belief that "the righteous shall be publicly acquitted by **Christ** the Judge and admitted to everlasting life and glory, and the wicked be sentenced to everlasting punishment" (as quoted in Boutell, 1896, p. 273, emp. added).

Such allusions could be multiplied many times over. A quick glance at the extracurricular activities of several of the signers of the *Constitution* should be sufficient to cinch the point. Alexander Hamilton proposed the formation of the Christian Constitutional Society to promote Christian government to other countries

(1979, 25:605-610). James McHenry was the president of the Baltimore Bible Society (Steiner, 1921, p. 12). Rufus King was selected to serve as manager of the American Bible Society (1900, 6:28-30). Robert Treat Paine served as a military chaplain in 1755 (1992, 1:300). Charles Pinckney was president of the Charleston Bible Society (*Eighth Report…*, 1816). John Langdon served as vice-president of the American Bible Society (*Constitution of the American…*, 1816). Abraham Baldwin was a chaplain in the American Revolution for two years (Thompson, 1978, 1:246). It is a fact: Christianity was the religion of the Founders.

James McHenry   Rufus King   Robert Treat Paine

Charles Pinckney   John Langdon   Abraham Baldwin

THE PLEDGE OF ALLEGIANCE

Though the Pledge of Allegiance was written in 1892, it did not contain the words "under God" until they were added in 1954 by none other than—Congress ("Congress Confirms...," 2002). Apparently this thoroughly political body was completely ignorant and uninformed regarding the alleged necessity of separation of church and state. The President at the time, Dwight D. Eisenhower, in a message delivered in Louisville, Kentucky on August 17, 1954, expressed American sentiments at the time regarding the words "under God":

> These words will remind Americans that despite our great physical strength we must remain humble. They will help us to keep constantly in our minds and hearts the spiritual and moral principles which alone give dignity to man, **and upon which our way of life is founded** ("Dwight David...," n.d., emp. added).

Dwight Eisenhower

The Pledge continues to come under attack in the ongoing attempts to expel God from public life. It has been declared unconstitutional by both the 9th Circuit Court of Appeals ("Lawmakers…," 2002) and a U.S. District Court judge ("Federal Judge…," 2005). In 2002, both houses of the U.S. Congress (by a vote of 401-5 in the House of Representatives and 99-0 in the Senate) reaffirmed the inclusion of "under God" ("Congress Confirms...," 2002). So far, the U.S. Supreme Court has refrained from weighing in on the constitutionality of requiring pupils to recite the pledge. Nevertheless, "under God" remains a part of the Pledge as formally designated in the U.S. Code, Title 4, Chapter 1, Section 4 (see *United States Code Online*).

THE NATIONAL MOTTO

"In God We Trust" remains the official national motto of the nation, as stipulated in the *United States Code*, TITLE 36, Subtitle I, Part A, Chapter 3, Section 302 (see *United States Code Online*). Again, due to ongoing threats of judicial tyranny, in 2002 both houses of the U.S. Congress also reaffirmed the words as the national motto ("Congress Confirms...").

NATIONAL SONGS

FRANCIS SCOTT KEY.

Many songs and hymns have come to characterize our national consciousness, even to the point of being intertwined with political expression. Francis Scott Key, 35-year-old poet-lawyer, was aboard ship on September 13, 1814 eight miles away when he witnessed the valiant defense of Fort McHenry by American forces during the British bombardment in the war of 1812. The incident inspired him to write the words to "The Star-Spangled Banner." He later stated: "Then, in that hour of deliverance, my heart spoke. Does not such a country, and such defenders of their country, deserve a song?" ("Fort McHenry..."). Though written in 1814, it was not until 1931 that the song was adopted by Congress as the official national anthem. Few Americans are aware that the fourth verse reaffirms the historic national attitude toward God:

Oh! thus be it ever, when freemen shall stand

Between their loved homes and the war's desolation!

Blest with victory and peace, **may the heaven-rescued land**

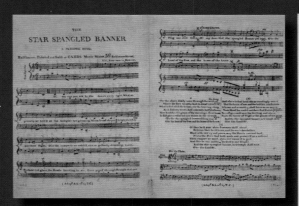

Praise the Power that hath made and preserved us a nation.

Then conquer we must, when our cause it is just,

And this be our motto: "**In God is our trust**."

And the star-spangled banner in triumph shall wave

O'er the land of the free and the home of the brave!

"God of our Fathers" was selected as the official hymn of the Centennial observance commemorating the adoption of the *Constitution* (Smith, 2000). The lyrics reaffirm national sentiments regarding the role of God and the one true religion in America's history:

God of our fathers, **Whose almighty hand** leads forth in beauty all the starry band

Of shining worlds in splendor through the skies Our grateful songs **before Thy throne** arise.

Thy love divine hath led us in the past, In this free land **by Thee** our lot is cast,

Be Thou our Ruler, Guardian, Guide and Stay, **Thy Word** our law, **Thy paths** our chosen way.

Top Left: "The Star Spangled Banner" printed sheet music.
Top Right: "The Star Spangled Banner" in Francis Scott Key's own handwriting, 1840.
Courtesy of the Music Division, Library of Congress

Samuel Smith

From war's alarms, from deadly pestilence, Be **Thy strong arm** our ever sure defense;

Thy true religion in our hearts increase, **Thy bounteous goodness** nourish us in peace.

Refresh **Thy** people on their toilsome way, Lead us from night to never ending day;

Fill all our lives with love and grace divine, And **glory, laud, and praise be ever Thine**.

While studying at Andover Theological Seminary in 1831, Samuel Francis Smith wrote the song "My Country 'Tis of Thee," also known simply as "America" ("Patriotic Melodies"). Observe the fourth verse:

Our fathers' God, to thee, Author of liberty, to thee we sing;

Long may our land be bright with freedom's holy light.

Protect us by thy might, Great God our King.

It was during the American Civil War in 1861, while visiting a Union Army camp on the Potomac River near Washington, D.C., that Julia Ward Howe was motivated to write the "Battle Hymn of the Republic" ("Battle Hymn…"). The song is replete with allusions to Christianity:

Mine eyes have seen the glory of the coming of **the Lord**;

He is trampling out the vintage where the grapes of wrath are stored;

He hath loosed the fateful lightning of **His** terrible swift sword;

His truth is marching on.

I have seen **Him** in the watch fires of a hundred circling camps.

They have builded **Him** an altar in the evening dews and damps;

I can read **His righteous sentence** by the dim and flaring lamps;

His day is marching on.

I have read a fiery **Gospel** writ in burnished rows of steel;

"As ye deal with **My** contemners, so with you **My grace** shall deal";

Let the Hero, born of woman, crush the serpent with His heel

[*Genesis 3:15*],

Since **God** is marching on.

He has sounded forth the trumpet that shall never call retreat;

He is sifting out the hearts of men before **His judgment seat**;

Oh, be swift, my soul, to answer **Him**! be jubilant, my feet;

Our God is marching on.

In the beauty of the lilies **Christ was born across the sea**,

With a glory in **His bosom** that transfigures you and me:

As **He died to make men holy**, let us die to make men free;

While **God** is marching on.

He is coming like the glory of the morning on the wave,

He is wisdom to the mighty, **He is honor** to the brave;

So the world shall be **His footstool**, and the soul of wrong **His slave**,

Our God is marching on.

Glory! Glory! Hallelujah! Glory! Glory! Hallelujah!

Glory! Glory! Hallelujah! **Our God** is marching on.

Few today realize that "hallelujah" is Hebrew for "praise the Lord."

The words to "America the Beautiful" were written by Katharine Lee Bates in 1893, after an inspiring trip to the top of Pikes Peak, Colorado ("America the…"). It, too, acknowledges the historic national belief in and commitment to God:

Julia Ward Howe

O beautiful for spacious skies, for amber waves of grain,

For purple mountain majesties above the fruited plain!

America! America! **God shed His grace** on thee,

And crown thy good with brotherhood from sea to shining sea.

America! America! **God mend thine ev'ry flaw**,

Confirm thy soul in self-control, thy liberty in law.

America! America! **May God** thy gold refine

Till all success be nobleness, and ev'ry gain **divine**.

PUBLIC EXPRESSIONS OF GOD IN THE JUDICIARY

STATE SUPREME COURTS

The courts of America once openly avowed the nation's affiliation with the one true God and the one true religion. For example, in a case that came before the New York State Supreme Court in 1811, a man had been convicted by a lower court for the following offense:

> [H]e did on the 2nd day of September, 1810, at Salem, wickedly, maliciously, and blasphemously, utter, and with a loud voice publish, in the presence and hearing of divers good and **Christian people**, of and concerning **the Christian religion**, and of and concerning **Jesus Christ**, the false, scandalous, malicious, wicked and blasphemous words...in contempt of the **Christian religion**, and the laws of this State (*People v. Ruggles*, emp. added).

He was found guilty, sentenced to three months in prison, and fined $500. The man's attorney argued that Christianity was not a part of the laws of the State, and that the *Constitution* allowed a free toleration to all religions and all kinds of worship. Nevertheless, the State Supreme Court upheld the man's conviction. The opinion of the court was penned by one of the Fathers of American Jurisprudence, Chief Justice James Kent, whose *Commentaries on American Law* (1826) effectively supplanted Blackstone's *Commentaries* as the premier expression of American law:

> [W]hatever strikes at the root of **Christianity** tends manifestly to the **dissolution of civil government**.... The people of this State, in common with the people of this country, **profess the general doctrines of Christianity**, as the rule of their faith and practice; and **to scandalize the author of these doctrines** is not only, in a religious point of view, extremely impious, but, even in respect to the obligations due to society, is a gross violation of decency and good order.... [T]o revile, with malicious and blasphemous contempt, **the religion professed by almost the whole community**, is an abuse of that right. Nor are we bound, by any expressions in the constitution, as some have strangely supposed, either not to punish at all, or to punish indiscriminately the like attacks upon the religion of Mahomet or of the Grand Lama; and for this plain reason, that the case assumes that **we are a Christian people, and the morality of the country is deeply ingrafted upon Christianity, and not upon the doctrines or worship of those imposters** (*People v. Ruggles*, emp. added).

James Kent

Unbelievable! Not only did this Father of American Jurisprudence forcefully acknowledge the universal recognition that America's allegiance was to the **Christian** religion, he committed what would now be considered a grievous, politically incorrect blunder of seismic proportions: he condemned Islam (Muhammad) and Buddhism (the Dalai Lama) as **false** religions! Yet he was merely expressing the viewpoint of 99.9% of his fellow Americans.

In a case that came before the Supreme Court of Pennsylvania, the court declared America's unflinching attachment to the general precepts of the Christian religion:

> This is **the Christianity of the common law**, incorporated into the great law of Pennsylvania, and thus, it is irrefragably proved, that **the laws and institutions of this state are built on the foundation of reverence for Christianity**.... On this the constitution of the United States has made no alteration, nor in the great body of the laws which was an incorporation of the common law doctrine **of Christianity**, as suited to the condition of the colony, and **without which no free government can long exist**....

> No free government now exists in the world, **unless where Christianity is acknowledged, and is the religion of the country**.... **Christianity is part of the common law of this state**. It is not proclaimed by the commanding voice of any human superior, but expressed in the calm and mild accents of customary law. **Its foundations are broad, and strong, and**

deep: they are laid in the authority, the interest, the affections of the people.... [I]t is **the purest system of morality, the firmest auxiliary, and only stable support of all human laws** (*Updegraph*..., 1824, emp. added).

In a case that went before the Supreme Court of Maryland in 1799, the justices delivered a unanimous opinion, including the following then-typical affirmations:

> Religion is of general and public concern, and on its support depend, in great measure, the peace and good order of government, the safety and happiness of the people. **By our form of government, the Christian religion is the established religion**; and all sects and denominations **of Christians** are placed upon the same equal footing, and are equally entitled to protection in their religious liberty. The principles of the **Christian** religion cannot be diffused, and its doctrines generally propagated, without places of public worship, and teachers and ministers, to explain **the scriptures** to

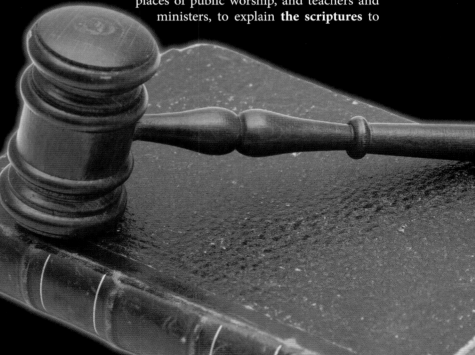

the people, and to enforce an observance of the precepts of religion by their preaching and living. And the pastors, teachers and ministers, of every denomination **of Christians**, are equally entitled to the protection of the law, and to the enjoyment of their religious and temporal rights (*Runkel...*, emp. added).

U.S. SUPREME COURT

In 1892, the United States Supreme Court issued a ruling in which the Court cited instance after instance, proof after proof, that from the very beginning America was closely aligned with the God of the Bible and the Christian religion. They brought their review of America's religious heritage to a close with this grand conclusion: "These, and many other matters which might be noticed, add a volume of unofficial declarations to the mass of organic utterances that **this is a Christian nation**" (*Church of the...*, emp. added).

The U.S. Supreme Court reaffirmed the same in 1931: "**We are a Christian people**...according to one another the equal right of religious freedom, and acknowledging with reverence the duty of obedience to **the will of God**" (*United States v...*, emp. added). How many Americans today realize that the U.S. Supreme Court has declared that America is a Christian nation? Many additional instances of the judiciary's support for the nation's Christian origins could be cited.

PUBLIC EXPRESSIONS OF GOD ON CURRENCY

In November of 1861, Salmon P. Chase, Secretary of the Treasury under Abraham Lincoln, issued the following directive to the Director of the Mint in Philadelphia:

> No nation can be strong **except in the strength of God** or safe **except in His defense. The trust of our people in God** should be declared on our national coins. You will cause a device to be prepared without unnecessary delay with a motto expressing in the fewest and tersest words possible **this national recognition** ("History of 'In...,'" emp. added).

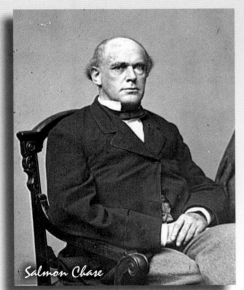

Salmon Chase

On April 22, 1864, by Act of Congress, the motto "In God we Trust" was approved for placement on American coins, beginning with the 1864 two-cent piece. Congress—a thoroughly political, governmental body—placed an unmitigated religious allusion on government-minted coinage! Apparently, the U.S. Government in 1864 understood neither the *Constitution* nor the so-called "separation of church and state." It took the creation of the ACLU to correct such "egregious errors" and provide us with a correct understanding of our *Constitution*.

Prior to 1864, manifestations of America's religious preference during the 18th century appeared on the Constellatio Nova copper coins. An eye emanating rays outward toward a surround-

ing circle of thirteen stars is historically identified as the Eye of Providence, symbolizing divine favor for the new nation ("The Nova...," n.d.). The same symbolism is on currency notes from the 1770s ("Continental Currency: 1779 $40..."). Other indications of America's religious heritage manifested on money include the $60 currency note from January 14, 1779. The emblem on the front shows a globe of the Earth with a motto from Psalm 97 in capital letters: "DEUS REGNAT EXULTET TERRA," i.e., "God reigns, let the Earth rejoice" ("Continental Currency: 1778..."). The 1779 $30 note has an emblem on the front showing a wreath on a tomb, with the motto: "SI RECTE FACIES"— "If you act righteously" ("Continental Currency: 1779 $30..."). Hence, religious references have been on America's money from the beginning.

PUBLIC EXPRESSIONS OF GOD ON NATIONAL SYMBOLS

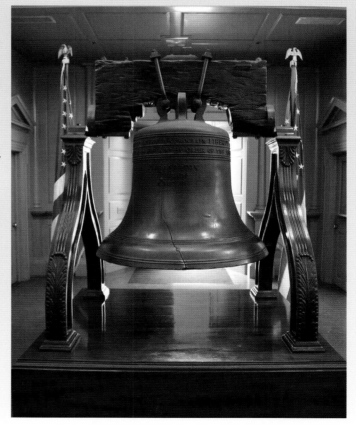

Several national symbols provide evidence of America's premiere attachment to the God of the Bible. Consider three. The Liberty Bell, cast in 1753, served as the official bell of the Pennsylvania State House. However, on July 8, 1776, it rang out to announce the first public reading of the *Declaration of Independence*. Since that day, it has served as a national symbol of liberty and is specially housed in Philadelphia near Independence Hall. Most Americans likely do not even realize that the words encircling the bell are taken from Leviticus 25:10—"Proclaim LIBERTY throughout all the land, unto all the inhabitants thereof" ("The Liberty...").

The Statue of Liberty stands on Bedloe's Island in New York harbor. On the fourth level at the base of the grand lady are seven jade-green, carrara-like, glass plaques, six of which have excerpts from works of great American statesmen ("Statue of Liberty..."). Inscribed on the seventh plaque is Leviticus 25:10—the same Bible verse that is on the Liberty Bell.

How many Americans are aware that we have a National Seal? On July 4, 1776, the Continental Congress assigned Benjamin Franklin, John Adams, and Thomas Jefferson the task of creating a seal for the United States of America. The seal was to embody the beliefs and values that the Founding Fathers wished to pass on to their descendents. Benjamin Franklin and Thomas Jefferson (again, two of the **least** religious of the Founders) proposed a thoroughly **biblical** design: Moses crossing the Red Sea, with Pharaoh in hot pursuit. It included the motto: "Rebellion to tyrants is obedience to God" ("The Great Seal..."; "Legend for the Seal...," 1998). These two men were so familiar with the Bible, and so believed in the God of the Bible, that they were able to draw the parallel between the relationship of the Israelites to Pharaoh and the relationship of Americans to the King of England. Observe further that both men viewed the separation from England to be **in accordance with the will of God**. As it turned out, their proposal did not make the cut.

The Great Seal was finalized and approved six years later on June 20, 1782. It has two sides. One side is sometimes referred to as the spiritual side. It contains a 13-step, incomplete pyramid with the year 1776 in Roman numerals at the base. At the top of the pyramid is a triangle (as if finishing out the pyramid) containing the Eye of Providence. Above the Eye is the motto *Annuit Coeptis*, which is Latin for "He (i.e., God) favors our undertakings" ("Symbols of U.S...."). Both sides of the Great Seal can be seen on the back of a one-dollar bill ("FAQs..."). That means that every dollar bill in America contains three allusions to the God of the Bible: "In God We Trust," the Eye of God, and "He favors our undertakings." ACLU attorneys must be pulling their hair out—though they continue to use the currency.

Left: 1856 drawing of the proposed Great Seal of the United States. Right: Benjamin Franklin's and Thomas Jefferson's holographic explanatory notes for the Seal, written on August 20, 1776. Courtesy of the Library of Congress

PUBLIC EXPRESSIONS OF GOD IN NATIONAL ARCHITECTURE

U.S. SUPREME COURT

Government buildings all over the country—from Washington, D.C. to the State capitols—are riddled with religious references, specifically to the God of the Bible and the Christian religion. Ironically, the United States Supreme Court building contains multiple allusions to the Ten Commandments. Directly above the Bench where the justices sit are two central figures, depicting Majesty of the Law and Power of Government. Between them is a tableau of the Ten Commandments ("Supreme Court..."). In three spots, as part of larger sculptural groups, Moses is depicted with tablets: on the exterior East Pediment, in the South Wall Courtroom frieze, and in one of the Great Hall metopes. Other tablets with the Roman numerals I-X appear on the support frame of the Courtroom's bronze gates as well as on the lower, interior panel of one of the oak doors that separate the Courtroom from the central hallway ("Symbols of Law")—**but Roy Moore could not display them in Alabama!**

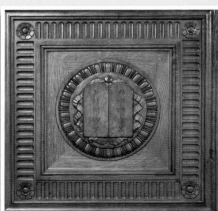

From left to right: Exterior East Pediment; South Wall Courtroom frieze; bronze gates support frame; Courtroom oak door
Courtesy of Collection of the Supreme Court of the United States

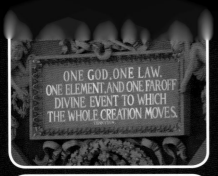

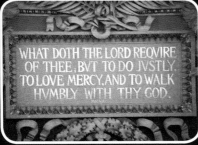

MOSES

Moving to the Library of Congress, eight large statues can be seen above the giant marble columns that surround the main reading room. They represent eight categories of knowledge, each considered symbolic of civilized life and thought. Above the figure of History are words from Lord Tennyson's *In Memoriam*: "ONE GOD, ONE LAW, ONE ELEMENT, AND ONE FAR-OFF DIVINE EVENT, TO WHICH THE WHOLE CREATION MOVES" ("On These Walls..."). Such words embody the Christian worldview and contradict atheism, Hinduism, Buddhism, and Native American religion. Above the figure of "Religion" are the words of Micah 6:8— "What doth the Lord require of thee, but to do justly, and to love mercy, and to walk humbly with thy God?" Above the figure of "Science" are the words of Psalm 19:1—"The heavens declare the glory of God; and the firmament sheweth His handiwork" ("On These Walls...").

Sixteen bronze statues set along the balustrade of the galleries, each pair flanking one of the eight giant marble columns, represent men renowned for their accomplishments in knowledge. The names of the individual figures are inscribed on the wall directly behind the statue. Representing "Religion" are the statues of the apostle Paul and Moses. Among the murals in the dome of the Main Reading Room are the words: "Thou shalt love thy neighbor as thyself. (Holy Bible, Leviticus 19:18)" inscribed in Hebrew. In the North Corridor is a painting called "Knowledge." The inscription reads: "Ignorance is the curse of God, knowledge the wing wherewith we fly to Heaven"—again, a clear expression of the Bible's teaching. Another quotation is taken directly from Proverbs 4:7—"Wisdom is the principal thing; therefore get wisdom; and with all thy getting, get understanding."

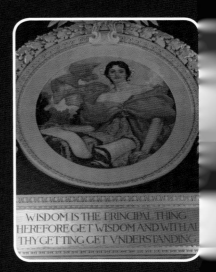

Also in the Library of Congress is the "Members of Congress Reading Room." Along the center of the ceiling are panels that represent civilization through the Spectrum of Light. Each of the seven panels features a central figure that symbolizes some phase of achievement, human or divine. The first subject is the creation of light with the words of Genesis 1:3—"Let there be light" ("On These Walls...," Part 1). In the ceiling vault of the West Corridor of the second floor of the Great Hall are the following quotations: "The First creature of God was the light of sense; the last was the light of reason" (from Bacon's Essays), as well as "The light shineth in darkness, and the darkness comprehendeth it not" from John 1:5. The South Corridor has a quote from Sir Thomas Browne: "Nature is the art of God" ("On These Walls...," Part 2).

U.S. CAPITOL

Moving to the U.S. Capitol complex, in the House Chamber, immediately above the American flag that is hung vertically on the wall behind the Speaker of the House, engraved in marble are the words: "In God We Trust" ("House of...," n.d.). Twenty-three marble relief portraits hang over the gallery doors of the House Chamber, depicting historical figures noted for their work in establishing the principles that underlie American law. Eleven profiles in the eastern half of the chamber face left and eleven in the western half face right, so that all 22 look towards the full-face relief of—Moses ("Relief Portraits...").

TONE

de MONTFORT

GAIUS

GROTIUS

INNOCENT III·

JEFFERSON

MAIMONIDES

NAPOLEON

AN

SOLON

SULEIMAN

ALFONSO X·

COLBERT

EDW

GREGORY IX

HAMMURABI

MOSES

JUSTINIAN

LYCURGUS

MASON

POTHIER

St·LOUIS

TRI

The House Rotunda doors show depictions of Christopher Columbus and his party **carrying a cross**. The Rotunda contains eight historical paintings, including Hernando DeSoto and Christopher Columbus, again, **carrying crosses**, the Protestant **baptism** of Pocahontas, and Protestant pilgrims aboard ship headed for America. The latter depicts Protestant pilgrims on the deck of their ship headed for the New World on July 22, 1620. William Brewster is holding **the Bible**, and John Robinson is leading Governor Carver, William Bradford, Miles Standish, and their families **in prayer**. The rainbow at the left side of the painting symbolizes hope and **divine protection** ("Works of Art..."). Also in the Capitol Rotunda is a 360-degree, painted, panoramic

Top: Christopher Columbus (first and second pictures on left); Hernando DeSoto (right).
Bottom, left to right: Christopher Columbus; Protestant baptism of Pocahontas; The Pilgrims.
Courtesy of Architect of the Capitol

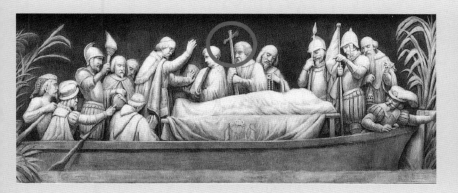

frieze, 58 feet above the floor, with 19 scenes depicting significant events in American history, beginning over the west door and moving clockwise around the Rotunda. These scenes include the burial of DeSoto (accompanied by **a cross**) and the landing of the Pilgrims with **Bible** in hand ("Frieze of American...").

Also in the Capitol is the Great Experiment Hall (the central east-west corridor) that chronicles in 16 murals three centuries of legislative milestones. The murals include George Washington and Abraham Lincoln taking the oath of office by placing their hands on **the Bible**, and a Protestant preacher symbolizing freedom of religion ("Works of Art...").

Top left: Burial of DeSoto. Top right: Landing of Pilgrims
Bottom, left to right: Washington taking oath of office; Lincoln's second inaugural; Freedom of religion in Protestant garb.
Courtesy of Architect of the Capitol

A stained glass window of George Washington praying on one knee is in the prayer room of the U.S. Capitol. Below him is "Psalm 16:1" with the words of the verse inscribed around him. "This Nation Under God" appears above him. At the top of the window is the Great Seal which, as noted previously, contains two allusions to God—the Providential Eye and *annuit coeptis* (Devorah, 2003). At the two lower left corners are an open Bible and a candle, symbolizing the light of God's Word ("U.S. Capitol Prayer Room," n.d.).

Courtesy of *Homeward Bound—The Journal of Ascended Master Devotion*

MISCELLANEOUS BUILDINGS

In the White House is situated the Adams Prayer Mantle which dates from 1800. The inscription constitutes an appeal to God: "I pray Heaven to bestow the best of blessings on this house and all that shall hereafter inhabit it. May none but honest and wise men ever rule under this roof" ("State Din-

Courtesy of the Library of Congress

ing Room..."). Images of the Ten Commandments are seen in a statue in front of the Ronald Reagan Building titled "Liberty of Worship," a sculpture in front of the U.S. District Court building (along with a cross), as well as embedded in the floor of the National Archives (Devorah, 2004). In 1961, two identical bronze plaques, that read "In God We Trust," were placed in the main lobby, east wall of the Longworth House Office Building, and at the southwest entrance, west wall of the Dirksen Office Building ("In God We...").

MEMORIALS

The Lincoln Memorial houses engravings of some of Lincoln's speeches. They, too, are punctuated with references to God and the Bible. For example, consider his second inaugural speech in which he addressed both sides of the Civil War [NOTE: Allusions to God and the Bible are noted in bold, and direct biblical citations are italicized and bracketed]:

Images on left: © Carrie Devorah, "God in the Temples of Government," All Rights Reserved.

Both read the same Bible, and pray to the same God; and each invokes his aid against the other. It may seem strange that any men should dare to ask **a just God's assistance** in wringing their bread from the sweat of other men's faces; but **let us "judge not, that we be not judged"** [*Matthew 7:1*]. The prayers of both could not be answered—that of neither has been answered fully. **The Almighty has his own purposes. "Woe unto the world because of offenses! for it must needs be that offenses come; but woe to that man by whom the offense cometh"** [*Matthew 18:7*].

If we shall suppose that American slavery is one of those offenses which, in **the providence of God**, must needs come, but which, having continued through **his** appointed time, **he** now wills to remove, and that **he** gives to both North and South this terrible war, as the woe due to those by whom the offense came, shall we discern therein any departure from **those divine attributes which the believers in a living God always ascribe to him**? Fondly do we hope—fervently do we pray—that this mighty scourge of war may speedily pass away. Yet, **if God wills** [*James 4:15*] that it continue until all the wealth piled by the bondsman's two hundred and fifty years of unrequited toil shall be sunk, and until every drop of blood drawn by the lash shall be paid by another drawn with the sword, as was said three thousand years ago, so still it must be said, **"The judgments of the Lord are true and righteous altogether"** [*Psalm 19:9*].

With malice toward none; with charity for all; with firmness in the right, **as God gives us** to see the right, let us strive on to finish the work we are in; to bind up the nation's wounds; to care for him who shall have borne the battle, and for his widow, and his orphan—to do all which may achieve and cherish a just and lasting peace among ourselves, and with all nations ("Lincoln...," emp., italics, and bracketed material added).

Also inscribed within the Lincoln Memorial is the Gettysburg Address which speaks of "this nation under God." Most Americans assume that it was Lincoln who coined the then historically apropos phrase: "A house divided against itself cannot stand." Yet he was merely quoting the Bible—Mark 3:25.

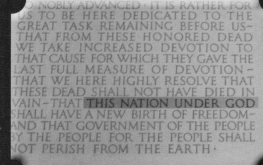

LINCOLN MEMORIAL

The Jefferson Memorial contains engravings from some of Jefferson's works, including numerous references to the God of the Bible:

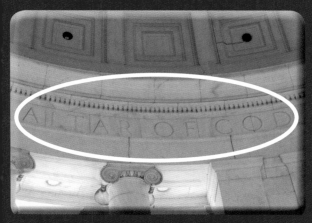

I have sworn upon **the altar of God** eternal hostility against every form of tyranny over the mind of man.

Almighty God hath created the mind free. All attempts to influence it by temporal punishments or burthens...are a departure from the plan of **the Holy Author of our religion**.... I know but **one code of morality for men** whether acting singly or collectively.

God who gave us life gave us liberty. Can the liberties of a nation be secure when we have removed a conviction that these liberties are **the gift of God**? Indeed I tremble for my country when I reflect that **God is just, that his justice cannot sleep forever** ("Thomas Jefferson Memorial...," emp. added).

Also located in the Jefferson Memorial are excerpts from the *Declaration of Independence* that include two of the four references to God found within that document.

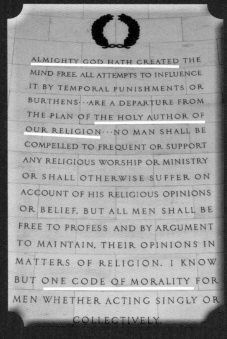

ALMIGHTY GOD HATH CREATED THE MIND FREE. ALL ATTEMPTS TO INFLUENCE IT BY TEMPORAL PUNISHMENTS OR BURTHENS···ARE A DEPARTURE FROM THE PLAN OF THE HOLY AUTHOR OF OUR RELIGION···NO MAN SHALL BE COMPELLED TO FREQUENT OR SUPPORT ANY RELIGIOUS WORSHIP OR MINISTRY OR SHALL OTHERWISE SUFFER ON ACCOUNT OF HIS RELIGIOUS OPINIONS OR BELIEF, BUT ALL MEN SHALL BE FREE TO PROFESS AND BY ARGUMENT TO MAINTAIN, THEIR OPINIONS IN MATTERS OF RELIGION. I KNOW BUT ONE CODE OF MORALITY FOR MEN WHETHER ACTING SINGLY OR COLLECTIVELY.

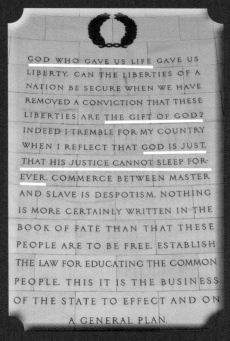

GOD WHO GAVE US LIFE GAVE US LIBERTY. CAN THE LIBERTIES OF A NATION BE SECURE WHEN WE HAVE REMOVED A CONVICTION THAT THESE LIBERTIES ARE THE GIFT OF GOD? INDEED I TREMBLE FOR MY COUNTRY WHEN I REFLECT THAT GOD IS JUST, THAT HIS JUSTICE CANNOT SLEEP FOREVER. COMMERCE BETWEEN MASTER AND SLAVE IS DESPOTISM. NOTHING IS MORE CERTAINLY WRITTEN IN THE BOOK OF FATE THAN THAT THESE PEOPLE ARE TO BE FREE. ESTABLISH THE LAW FOR EDUCATING THE COMMON PEOPLE. THIS IT IS THE BUSINESS OF THE STATE TO EFFECT AND ON A GENERAL PLAN.

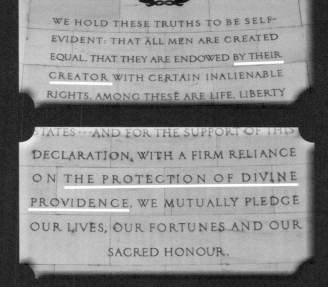

WE HOLD THESE TRUTHS TO BE SELF-EVIDENT: THAT ALL MEN ARE CREATED EQUAL, THAT THEY ARE ENDOWED BY THEIR CREATOR WITH CERTAIN INALIENABLE RIGHTS, AMONG THESE ARE LIFE, LIBERTY

STATES···AND FOR THE SUPPORT OF THIS DECLARATION, WITH A FIRM RELIANCE ON THE PROTECTION OF DIVINE PROVIDENCE, WE MUTUALLY PLEDGE OUR LIVES, OUR FORTUNES AND OUR SACRED HONOUR.

JEFFERSON MEMORIAL

The apex of the Washington Memorial is topped by a 100 ounce aluminum capstone that has on its east face two lone Latin words: *Laus Deo*, i.e., praise be to God ("The Washington..."; "Laus Deo"). Ascending the internal stairway, one can see 190 memorial stones donated by various states, cities, churches, and civic organizations during the 19th-century phase of construction. The stones abound with references to God, the Bible, Christianity, and Christian morality. For example, the stone donated by the state of Kentucky reads: "Under the Auspices of Heaven and the Precepts of Washington." The stone donated by the city of Baltimore reads: "May Heaven to This Union Continue Its Beneficence." Using biblical imagery (i.e., "ark," "covenant," "dove"), one city in Maryland linked the religion of the Pilgrims with the **birthright** of America in the memorial stone they contributed:

From the City of Frederick, Md. Civil and Religious Liberty first proclaimed in the Pilgrim Fathers of Maryland as emblemed in the Ark of the Covenant of Freedom, and the Dove, the Harbinger of Peace and fellowship that guided them though the danger of the deep, have been secured in the Birthright of the Nation by the enduring Seal of the Minister of Justice, George Washington ("Washington Monument...").

In addition to the apex and these memorial stones, many artifacts were deposited in the recess of the cornerstone after completion, including 71 newspapers that ran articles commemorating Washington, and a host of other historical objects—a veritable treasure trove of history. However, only one is religious in nature: the Bible ("Appendix C: Members...").

WASHINGTON MEMORIAL

PUBLIC EXPRESSIONS OF GOD IN EDUCATION

The public school system of today differs radically from the public education of America's early days. For all practical purposes, God and the Bible have now been banned from public schools, and Christian connections have been largely purged. What a far cry from early American schools, where **the religious and moral education of youth was paramount**. It is a historical fact that the Bible was the central focus of American education from the very beginning. It was the first book in the classroom. The Bible was used, not only to teach content, but to teach a child how to read, memorize, recite, and even write ("The Story of…," 2001).

New England Primer

The first textbook in the American school room was the *New England Primer*, extremely popular throughout the 1700s and 1800s. It was replete with Christian and biblical content (*New England…*, 1805). For example, page two of the 1805 edition has "A Divine Song of Praise to God, for a Child." Page 11 gives "Agur's Prayer," taken directly from Proverbs 30:8-9, and "Duty of

THE
NEW-ENGLAND
PRIMER
IMPROVED,

For the more easy attaining the true Reading of English.

ADORNED WITH CUTS.

TO WHICH IS ADDED,

THE ASSEMBLY OF DIVINES'
CATECHISM.

ALBANY:—Printed by
WHITING, BACKUS & WHITING,
And sold Wholesale and Retail at their Store,
No. 45, STATE-STREET.
1805.

(2)

A Divine Song of praise to God, for a Child by the Rev. Dr. Watts.

HOW glorious is our heav'nly King,
  Who reigns above the sky!
How shall a child presume to sing
  His dreadful Majesty!
How great his power is, none can tell,
  Nor think how large his grace,
Nor men below, nor saints that dwell
  On high before his face.

New England Primer
Courtesy of Special Collections, Gettysburg College, Gettysburg, Pennsylvania

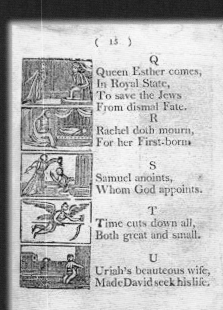

Children towards their Parents," which simply quotes Matthew 15:4 and Ephesians 6:1. Pages 12-16 teach the alphabet using rhymed references to the Bible, including: "B—Thy life to mend, this Book attend"; "P—Peter denies, his Lord and cries"; "Q—Queen Esther comes, in Royal State, to save the Jews, from dismal Fate"; "R—Rachel doth mourn, for her First-born"; "S—Samuel anoints, whom God appoints"; "U—Uriah's beauteous wife, made David seek his life"; "Z—Zaccheus he, did climb the tree, his Lord to see." Page 17 offers "Moral Precepts for Children" followed by "The Lord's Prayer." Pages 19-21 have "A Cradle Hymn, by Dr. Watts" with numerous references to Christ. Page 21 has the familiar bedtime rhyme: "Now I lay me down to sleep, I pray thee, Lord, my soul to keep; If I should die before I wake, I pray thee, Lord, my soul to take." This rhyme is followed by: "Good Children must: Fear God all day, parents obey, no false thing say, by no sin stray, love Christ alway, in secret pray, mind little play, make no delay, in doing good." Pages 22-29 recount the death of John Rodgers, "minister of the gospel," who "died courageously for the gospel of Jesus Christ" at the hands of a Catholic queen. Pages 30-56 offer "The Shorter Catechism" consisting of scores of questions and answers from the Bible, concluding with "Some short and easy Questions":

Q: Who made you? A: God

Q: Who redeemed you? A: Jesus Christ

Q: Who sanctifies and preserves you?   A: The Holy Ghost

Q: Of what are you made? A: Dust

Q: What doth that teach you? A: To be humble and mindful of death.

New England Primer
Courtesy of Special Collections, Gettysburg College, Gettysburg, Pennsylvania

Q: For what end was [sic] you made? A: To serve God

Q: How must you serve Him? A: In spirit and in truth [*John 4:24*]

From pages 57-67, the student was treated to "A Dialogue Between Christ, a Youth, and the Devil" in which a child is encouraged to make the right moral decisions in life in preparation for death. Pages 68-70 consist of "Questions and Answers out of the Holy Scriptures." Page 71 has "A short Prayer to be used every Morning" and "A short prayer to be used every Evening"—the very thing banned by the U.S. Supreme Court in the 1960s. The final page (p. 72) closes with a poem that concludes with 1 Corinthians 15:55. This premiere American public school textbook is so thoroughly saturated with Bible teaching that it could just as easily be used in a church's Sunday morning Bible class!

BLUE-BACK SPELLER

Another significant American public school textbook, Noah Webster's *The American Spelling Book* published in 1787, revised in 1829 and renamed *The Elementary Spelling Book* (nicknamed "Blue-Back Speller"), dominated public education from the late 1700s through the Civil War, "selling some 70 million copies into the 20th century" (Monaghan, 2002, 25[2]; cf. Monaghan, 1983). It, too, is literally laced with references to God, the Bible, Christianity, and Christian moral principles—all now deemed politically incor-

rect and unconstitutional. For example, the following sample sentences were designed to develop the student's ability to read, pronounce, and build vocabulary [NOTE: Direct biblical citation is in bold and bracketed]:

A rude girl will romp in the street (p. 24).

Good boys and girls will act well (p. 24).

The Holy Bible is the book of God (p. 26).

To filch is to steal. We must not filch (p. 27).

Strong drink will debase a man (p. 28). **[Proverbs 20:1]**

Teachers like to see their pupils polite to each other (p. 28).

Good men obey the laws of God (p. 29).

God created the heavens and the earth in six days, and all that was made was very good (p. 29). **[Genesis 1:31]**

We go to church on the first day of the week (p. 30).

God will bless those who do his will (p. 32).

The preacher is to preach the gospel (p. 41).

Blasphemy is contemptuous treatment of God (p. 42).

Litany is a solemn service of prayer to God (p. 42).

Felony is a crime that may be punished with death (p. 42).

That idle boy is a very lazy fellow (p. 44).

God made the ear, and He can hear (p. 46). **[Psalm 94:9]**

The gambler wishes to get money without earning it (p. 49).

Men devoted to mere amusement misemploy their time (p. 50).

Washington was not a selfish man. He labored for the good of his country more than for himself (p. 50).

We punish bad men to prevent crimes (p. 51).

The drunkard's face will publish his vice and his disgrace (p. 51).

The devil is the great adversary of man (p. 52). **[1 Peter 5:8]**

Labor makes us strong and healthy (p. 58).

A vagrant is a wandering, lazy fellow (p. 58).

We are apt to live forgetful of our continual dependence on the will of God (p. 66).

The drunkard's course is progressive; he begins by drinking a little, and shortens his life by drinking to excess (p. 67).

---

28 — THE ELEMENTARY

BĀR, LĂST, CĂRE, FĂLL, WHĂT; BĒR, PRĔY, THĔRE; GĚT; BĪRD, MĂRĪNE; LĬNK;

No. 32.—XXXII.

WORDS OF TWO SYLLABLES, ACCENTED ON THE SECOND.

a bāse'	re claim'	un say'	ben zoin'
de base	pro claim	as say	a void
in ease	dis claim	a way	a droit
a bate	ex claim	o bey	ex ploit
de bate	de mean	con vey	de coy
se date	be moan	pur vey	en joy
ere ate	re tain	sur vey	al loy
ob late	re main	de fy	em ploy
re late	en gross	af fy	an noy
in flate	dis creet	de ny	de stroy
eol late	al lay	de cry	con voy
trans late	de lay	re boil	es pouse
mis state	re lay	de spoil	ea rouse
re plete	in lay	em broil	de vour
com plete	mis lay	re coil	re dound
se crete	dis play	sub join	de vout
re cite	de cay	ad join	a mount
in cite	dis may	re join	sur mount
po lite	de fray	en join	dis mount
ig nite	ar ray	con join	re count
re deem	be tray	dis join	re nown
es teem	por tray	mis join	en dow
de claim	a stray	pur loin	a vow

Strong drink will debase a man.

Hard shells incase clams and oysters.

Men inflate balloons with gas, which is lighter than common air.

Teachers like to see their pupils polite to each other.

Idle men often delay till to-morrow things that should be done to-day.

SPELLING BOOK. — 29

Good men obey the laws of God.

I love to survey the starry heavens.

Careless girls mislay their things.

The fowler decoys the birds into his net.

Cats devour rats and mice.

The adroit ropedancer can leap and jump and perform as many exploits as a monkey.

Wise men employ their time in doing good to all around them.

In the time of war, merchant vessels sometimes have a convoy of ships of war.

Kings are men of high renown,

Who fight and strive, to wear a crown.

God created the heavens and the earth in six days, and all that was made was very good.

To purloin is to steal.

No. 33.—XXXIII.

deed	breed	glee	steel	green	sleek
feed	seed	free	deem	seen	meek
heed	weed	tree	seem	teen	reek
bleed	bee	eel	teem	steen	creek
meed	fee	feel	sheen	queen	Greek
need	see	heel	keen	ween	seek
speed	lee	peel	spleen	leek	week
reed	flee	reel	screen	cheek	beef

No. 34.—XXXIV.

deep	weep	leer	lees	meet	brood
sheep	sweep	fleer	bees	greet	geese
keep	beer	sneer	beet	street	fleece
sleep	deer	peer	feet	sweet	sleeve
peep	cheer	seer	sheet	food	reeve
creep	sheer	steer	fleet	mood	breeze
steep	jeer	queer	sleet	rood	freeze

Children should answer questions politely (p. 68).

God governs the world in infinite wisdom; the Bible teaches us that it is our duty to worship Him (p. 69).

It is a solemn thing to die and appear before God (p. 69).

Children should respect and obey their parents (p. 70). **[Ephesians 6:1]**

Satan afflicted Job with sore boils (p. 72). **[Job 2:7]**

"If sinners entice thee, consent thou not," **[Proverbs 1:10]** but withdraw from their company (p. 72). **[2 Thess. 3:6]**

The chewing of tobacco is a useless habit (p. 74).

We should be attentive and helpful to strangers (p. 75). **[Hebrews 13:2]**

Parents deserve the kind treatment of children (p. 75).

Prayer is a duty… (p. 75).

Confess your sins and forsake them (p. 76). **[Proverbs 23:10]**

The wicked transgress the laws of God (p. 76).

Before you rise in the morning or retire at night, give thanks to God for his mercies, and implore the continuance of his protection (p. 79).

The laws of nature are sustained by the immediate presence and agency of God (p. 80).

The Heavens declare an Almighty power that made them (p. 80). **[Psalm 19:1]**

How can a young man cleanse his way? (p. 82). **[Psalm 119:9]**

Oh, how love I Thy law! (p. 82). **[Psalm 119:97]**

Let us lay up for ourselves treasure in heaven, where neither moth nor rust can corrupt (p. 88). **[Matthew 6:20]**

Humility is the prime ornament of the Christian (p. 91).

---

72   THE ELEMENTARY

BĀR, LĀST, CĀRE, FALL, WHAT; HĒR, PREY, THĒRE; ĠET; BĪRD, MARĪNE; LĪNK;

e vĕnt	eom plāint'	ae eount'	be lōw'
re prĭnt	re straint	al low	be stōw
pre tĕxt	eon straint	en dow	af frŏnt
re lāx	dis traint	ba shaw	eon frŏnt
per plĕx	ae quaint	be dew	re prŏve
an nĕx	ap point	es chew	dis prŏve
de vour	dis joint	re new	im prŏve
a loud	a noint	fōre shōw	re plȳ

Heavy clouds foretell a shower of rain.
The rattan is a long slender reed that grows in Java.
Good children will submit to the will of their parents.
Let all your precepts be succinct and clear.
We elect men to make our laws for us.
Idle children neglect their books when young, and thus reject their advantages.
The little busy bees collect honey from flowers; they never neglect their employment.
The neck connects the head with the body.
Children should respect and obey their parents.
Parents protect and instruct their children.
Satan afflicted Job with sore boils.
The lady instructs her pupils how to spell and read.
Teachers should try to implant good ideas in the minds of their pupils.
The kind mother laments the death of a dear infant.
A bashaw is a title of honor among the Turks; a governor. The word is now commonly spelled *pasha*.
"If sinners entice thee, consent thou not," but withdraw from their company.

No. 87.—LXXXVII.

WORDS OF TWO SYLLABLES, ACCENTED ON THE FIRST.

fĭs' eal	pĭt' eoal	mĕn' tal	tĭm' brel
ŏf fal	mŏr al	mŏr tal	mŏn grel
fōrm al	çĕn tral	vĕs tal	quar rel
dĭs mal	văs sal	rev el	squĭr rel
chär eōal	dĕn tal	găm brel	mĭn strel

---

80   THE ELEMENTARY

BĀR, LĀST, CĀRE, FALL, WHAT; HĒR, PREY, THĒRE; ĠET; BĪRD, MARĪNE; LĪNK;

un sōwn	a light	a wāit	eon tour
a dȯ	de light	de çēit	be sīdes
out dȯ	a right	eon çēipt	re çēipt
a gō	af fright	a mȯur	re liēve

When the moon passes between the earth and the sun, we call it new; but you must not think that it is more new at that time, than it was when it was full; we mean, that it begins anew to show us the side on which the sun shines.
God ordained the sun to rule the day; and the moon and stars to give light by night.
The laws of nature are sustained by the immediate presence and agency of God.
The heavens declare an Almighty power that made them.
The science of astronomy explains the causes of day and night, and why the sun, and moon, and stars appear to change their places in the heavens.
Air contains the vapors that rise from the earth; and it sustains them, till they fall in dews, and in showers of rain, or in snow or hail.
Grapevines entwine their tendrils round the branches of trees.
Laws are made to restrain the bad, and protect the good.
Glue will make pieces of wood adhere.
The careful ant prepares food for winter.
We often compare childhood to the morning: morning is the first part of the day, and childhood is the first stage of human life.
Do not postpone till to-morrow what you should do to-day.
A harpoon is an instrument for striking whales.
Monsoon is a wind in the East Indies, that blows six months from one quarter, and then six months from another.
Be careful to keep your house in good repair.
Refrain from all evil; keep no company with immoral men.
Never complain of unavoidable calamities.
Let all your words be sincere, and never deceive.
A poltroon is an arrant coward, and deserves the contempt of all brave men.
Never practice deceit, for this is sinful.
To revere a father, is to regard him with fear mingled with respect and affection.
Brevier is a small kind of printing letter.

---

82   THE ELEMENTARY

MŌVE, SŎN, WŎLF, WŌOT, MŌON, ŌR; RULE, FULL; EXIST;

Gage is a French word, and signifies to pledge.
The banks engage to redeem their notes with specie, and they are obliged to fulfill their engagements.
To preëngage means to engage beforehand.
I am not at liberty to purchase goods which are preengaged to another person.
To disengage, is to free from a previous engagement.
A mediator is a third person who interposes to adjust a dispute between parties at variance.
How can a young man cleanse his way?
Oh, how love I Thy law!

No. 94.—XCIV.

WORDS OF THREE SYLLABLES, ACCENTED ON THE FIRST, LEFT UNMARKED FOR EXERCISE IN NOTATION.

NOUNS.	NOUNS.	ADJECTIVES.
cin' na mon	por' rin ger	du' te ous
et y mon	stom a cher	a que ous
grid i ron	ob se quies	du bi ous
and i ron	prom i ses	te di ous
skel e ton	com pass es	o di ous
sim ple ton	in dex es	stu di ous
buf fa lo	am ber gris	co pi ous
cap ri corn	em pha sis	ca ri ous
cal i co	di o cese	se ri ous
in di go	o li o	glo ri ous
ver ti go	o ver plus	cu ri ous
cal i ber	pu is sance	fu ri ous
bed cham ber	nu cle us	spu ri ous
cin na bar	ra di us	li mi nous
of fi cer	ter mi nus	glu ti nous
col an der	blun der buss	mu ti nous
lav en der	syl la bus	ru in ous
prov en der	in cu bus	lu di crous
cyl in der	ver bi age	dan ger ous
in te ger	Sir i us	hid e ous
scav en ger	cal a mus	in fa mous
har bin ger	mit ti mus	ster to rous

SPELLING BOOK.   91

MŌVE, SŎN, WŎLF, WŌOT, MŌON, ŌR; RŪLE, FŬLL; EXIST; ĢEM; ÇEM, CHAISE.

re al' i ty	de spond' en cy	hy poc' ri sy
le gal i ty	e mer gen cy	ti moc ra cy
re gal i ty	in clem en cy	im pi e ty
fru gal i ty	con sist en cy	va ri e ty
for mal i ty	in solv en cy	e bri e ty
car nal i ty	de lin quen cy	so bri e ty
neu tral i ty	mo not o ny	pro pri e ty
as cend an cy	a pos ta sy	sa ti e ty

The winters in Lapland are severe. The people of that country dress in furs, to protect themselves from the severity of the cold.
Major signifies more or greater; minor means less.
A majority is more than half; a minority is less than half.
Plurality denotes two or more; as, a plurality of worlds.
In grammar, the plural number expresses more than one; as, two men, ten boys.
A majority of votes means more than half of them.
When we say a man has a plurality of votes, we mean he has more than any one else.
Members of Congress and Assembly are often elected by a plurality of votes.
Land is valued for its fertility and nearness to market.
Many parts of the United States are noted for the fertility of the soil.
The rapidity of a stream sometimes hinders its navigation.
Consistency of character, in just men, is a trait that commands esteem.
Humility is the prime ornament of a Christian.

No. 102.—CII.

WORDS OF FIVE SYLLABLES, ACCENTED ON THE SECOND.

eo tem' po ra ry	de elam' a to ry
ex tem po ra ry	ex elam a to ry
de rŏg a to ry	in flam ma to ry
ap pel la to ry	ex plan a to ry
eon sōl a to ry	de elar a to ry
de fam a to ry	pre par a to ry

A love of trifling amusements is derogatory to the Christian character (p. 92).

Christian humility is never derogatory to character (p. 92).

God is the divine legislator… (p. 98).

It is the duty of every good man to inspect the moral conduct of the man who is offered as a legislator at our yearly elections. If the people wish for good laws, they may have them, by electing good men (pp. 98-99).

Noah and his family outlived all the people who lived before the flood (p. 101). [Genesis 8:18]

God will forgive those who repent of their sins, and live a holy life (p. 101).

Thy testimonies, O Lord, are very sure; holiness becometh thine house forever (p. 101). [Psalm 93:5]

Do not attempt to deceive God; nor to mock him with solemn words whilst your heart is set to do evil (p. 101).

A holy life will disarm death of its sting (p. 101). [1 Corinthians 15:56]

God will impart grace to the humble penitent (p. 101). [1 Peter 5:5]

Abusive words irritate the passions, but "a soft answer turneth away wrath" (p. 104). [Proverbs 15:1]

Good manners are always becoming; ill manners are evidence of low breeding (p. 105).

The heathen are those people who worship idols, or who know not the true God (p. 115).

Those who enjoy the light of the gospel, and neglect to observe its precepts, are more criminal than the heathen (p. 115).

It is every man's duty to bequeath to his children a rich inheritance of pious precepts (p. 115).

Bad boys sometimes know what a whip is by their feelings. This is a kind of knowledge which good boys dispense with (p. 120).

"Take away your exactions from my people." Ezek. xiv.9. (p. 121).

Examine the Scriptures daily and carefully, and set an example of good works (p. 121). [Acts 17:11; Titus 2:7]

The Bible, that is, the Old and the New Testament, contains the Holy Scriptures (p. 135).

Whatever is wrong is a deviation from right, or from the just laws of God or man (p. 136).

How happy men would be if they would always love what is right and hate what is wrong (p. 136). [Amos 5:15]

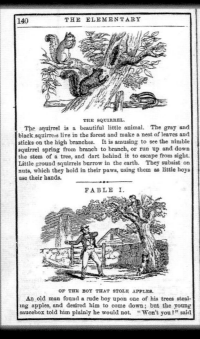

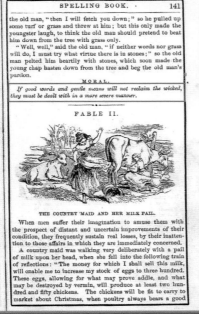

This volume also contains several fables that teach a variety of lessons. Consider Fable 1, titled "Of the Boy that Stole Apples":

> An old man found a rude boy upon one of his trees stealing apples, and desired him to come down; but the young saucebox told him plainly he would not. "Won't you?" said the old man, "then I will fetch you down;" so he pulled up some turf or grass and threw at him; but this only made the youngster laugh, to think the old man should pretend to beat him down from the tree with grass only.

> "Well, well," said the old man, "if neither words nor grass will do, I must try what virtue there is in stones;" so the old man pelted him heartily with stones, which soon made the young chap hasten down from the tree and beg the old man's pardon (pp. 140-141).

By today's standards, one would expect the outcome of this story to be that the police arrived on the scene, arrested and jailed the old man for injury to a child, followed by a civil suit filed by the boy's parents for child abuse, thereby destroying the old man's reputation and sending him into bankruptcy. In contrast, the book gives the following moral: "**If good words and gentle means will not reclaim the wicked, they must be dealt with in a more severe manner**" (p. 141).

Observe that a central purpose of the "Blue-Back Speller" was to instill in children proper conduct (i.e., what is courteous and polite vs. what is rude and socially unacceptable), moral integrity (evils of alcohol, lying, stealing, gambling, selfishness, laziness, etc.), true religion (worship, church, Bible, sin, etc.), and citizenship (patriotism, respect for the Founders, and love for God and country). Indeed, such truths and insights cultivate the soul, buoy the spirit, and prepare a child to lead a productive, disciplined, honorable life. In sharp contradistinction, the removal of these basic precepts from public education has had a catastrophic, deleterious effect on the moral sensibilities and social stability of the nation.

McGuffey's Readers

A third prominent source of public education was the *McGuffey's Reader*. First printed in 1836, the series consisted of six readers corresponding to six levels of difficulty. With some 120 million copies sold between 1836 and 1890, "[p]ractically every American who attended public schools during the second half of the nineteenth century learned moral and ethical lessons from *McGuffey's Reader*" ("McGuffey's Reader," 2005). These volumes, like those already noted, were riddled with a biblical worldview and the essentiality of Christian morality. In fact, in the Publisher's Preface to the "Parent/Teacher Guide," the President of Mott Media made the following insightful assessment of the views of McGuffey and the corresponding impact on American civilization:

Publisher's Preface

How would McGuffey teach reading if he were here today? First, he would be concerned about the content of pupils' reading. The content would promote moral growth and excellence of mind in habits, attitudes, and literary tastes. And morality, in McGuffey's thinking, was closely aligned with the Christian religion; no other foundation could produce true morality. Upon this basis he collected and wrote the selections for his famous Readers.

McGuffey believed in carefully adapting to the individuality of each child. He felt that parents often sent their dearest treasures off to school too early in life. No two minds are alike in all their powers and susceptibilities, he wrote. Therefore the mode of treatment should be somewhat different for each. Moving at the pupil's own pace helps to preserve the vigor and energy of his mental action. Memorizing forms a habit of attention, and this good attention helps a pupil understand and master even those studies which he does not memorize. Thus, memorizing should be used sometimes and understanding should be pursued at all times.

Having a wide vocabulary is one of the most obvious results of a cultivated mind, and the best way to grow such a vocabulary is to learn words in their context, as in studying a selection from the Readers. Teachers and pupils talk together about the important ideas and noble thoughts presented in the Readers. Pupils read, reread, write, and ask and answer questions, and through it all they adopt more and more words into their own repertoire of available and useful vocabulary.

For beginning reading, phonics is important. Children should be drilled on sounds before they begin reading and after they start reading. The McGuffey Primers and the McGuffey Speller help build for young children this kind of strong phonics foundation.

These and other McGuffey principles are found in this Teacher's Guide. We are happy to bring this help to you who are teaching reading the McGuffey way.

George M. Mott, President
Mott Media, Inc.

How would McGuffey teach reading if he were here today? First, he would be concerned about the content of pupils' reading. The content would promote moral growth and excellence of mind in habits, attitudes, and literary tastes. And **morality, in McGuffey's thinking, was closely aligned with the Christian religion; no other foundation could produce true morality** ("McGuffey Readers…," n.d., emp. added).

A quick perusal of the various tables of content demonstrates the point. [NOTE: Direct biblical citation is bolded and bracketed.] In the second reader (dated 1836), the readings include "Praise to God" (p. 77), "About Doing Good at Play" (p. 87), "The Honest Boy and the Thief" (p. 142), "The Lord's Prayer" [**Matthew 6:9-13**] (p. 162), "The Disobedient Girl" (p. 166), "Story about Joseph" [**Genesis 37-50**] (p. 198), "The Ten Commandments" [**Exodus 20:1-17**] (p. 229), and "About Using Profane Language" (p. 233). In the third reader (dated 1837), the listing includes "The Goodness of God" (p. 157), "Touch not—Taste not—Handle not" [**Colossians 2:21**] (p. 208), and "Gospel Invitation" (p. 238). The fourth reader (dated 1838) includes "Divine Providence" (p. 168), "Scripture Lesson" (p. 182), "Thirsting after Righteousness" [**Matthew 5:6**] (p. 216), "Satan and Death at the Gate of Hell" (p. 232), "Christian Hymn of Triumph…" (p. 309), and "The Proverbs of Solomon"

ECLECTIC EDUCATIONAL SERIES.

McGUFFEY'S

FIFTH

ECLECTIC READER.

REVISED EDITION.

NEW-YORK ❖ CINCINNATI ❖ CHICAGO

AMERICAN BOOK COMPANY

FROM THE PRESS OF
VAN ANTWERP, BRAGG, & CO.

CONTENTS

[**Proverbs**] (p. 411). The revised edition of the fifth reader includes "Respect for the Sabbath Rewarded" (p. 69), "Select Paragraphs" from the Bible (p. 72), "The Righteous Never Forsaken" [**Psalm 37:25**] (p. 92), "The Goodness of God" from the Bible (p. 167), "The Hour of Prayer" (p. 171), "Religion the only Basis of Society" (p. 284), "The Bible the Best of Classics" (p. 350), and "My Mother's Bible" (p. 351).

To see the extent to which the thinking that prevails in America in general, and public education in particular, has been significantly altered, take a moment to read the three pages written by William Ellery Channing, born during America's Founding era, on "Religion the only Basis of Society"—pages that would certainly not be included in any education textbook today, but which ought to cause us to tremble!

---

284   *ECLECTIC SERIES.*

10. And the warm sea's mellow murmur
      Resounding day and night;
      A thousand shapes and tints and tones
      Of manifold delight,

11. Nearer and ever nearer
      Drawing with every day!
      But a little longer to wait and watch
      'Neath skies so cold and gray;

12. And hushed is the roar of the bitter north
      Before the might of the Spring,
      And up the frozen slope of the world
      Climbs Summer, triumphing.

XCIII. RELIGION THE ONLY BASIS OF SOCIETY.

William Ellery Channing (*b.* 1780, *d.* 1842) an eminent divine and orator, was born at Newport, R. I. He graduated from Harvard with the highest honors in 1798, and, in 1803, he was made pastor of the Federal Street Church, Boston, with which he maintained his connection until his death. Towards the close of his life, being much enfeebled, he withdrew almost entirely from his pastoral duties, and devoted himself to literature. Dr. Channing's writings are published in six volumes, and are mainly devoted to theology.

1. RELIGION is a social concern; for it operates powerfully on society, contributing in various ways to its stability and prosperity. Religion is not merely a private affair; the community is deeply interested in its diffusion; for it is the best support of the virtues and principles, on which the social order rests. Pure and undefiled religion is, to do good; and it follows, very plainly, that if God be the Author and Friend of society, then, the recognition of him must enforce all social duty, and enlightened piety must give its whole strength to public order.

FIFTH READER.   285

2. Few men suspect, perhaps no man comprehends, the extent of the support given by religion to every virtue. No man, perhaps, is aware, how much our moral and social sentiments are fed from this fountain; how powerless conscience would become without the belief of a God; how palsied would be human benevolence, were there not the sense of a higher benevolence to quicken and sustain it; how suddenly the whole social fabric would quake, and with what a fearful crash it would sink into hopeless ruin, were the ideas of a Supreme Being, of accountableness and of a future life to be utterly erased from every mind.

3. And, let men thoroughly believe that they are the work and sport of chance; that no superior intelligence concerns itself with human affairs; that all their improvements perish forever at death; that the weak have no guardian, and the injured no avenger; that there is no recompense for sacrifices to uprightness and the public good; that an oath is unheard in heaven; that secret crimes have no witness but the perpetrator; that human existence has no purpose, and human virtue no unfailing friend; that this brief life is every thing to us, and death is total, everlasting extinction; once let them *thoroughly* abandon religion, and who can conceive or describe the extent of the desolation which would follow?

4. We hope, perhaps, that human laws and natural sympathy would hold society together. As reasonably might we believe, that were the sun quenched in the heavens, *our* torches would illuminate, and *our* fires quicken and fertilize the creation. What is there in human nature to awaken respect and tenderness, if man is the unprotected insect of a day? And what is he more, if atheism be true?

5. Erase all thought and fear of God from a community, and selfishness and sensuality would absorb the whole man. Appetite, knowing no restraint, and suffering, having no solace or hope, would trample in scorn on the restraints

---

286   *ECLECTIC SERIES.*

of human laws. Virtue, duty, principle, would be mocked and spurned as unmeaning sounds. A sordid self-interest would supplant every feeling; and man would become, in fact, what the theory in atheism declares him to be,—*a companion for brutes.*

DEFINITIONS.—1. Com-mū'ni-ty, *society at large, the public.* Dĭf-fū'ṣion, *extension, spread.* En-light'ened, *elevated by knowledge and religion.* 2. Făb'ric, *any system composed of connected parts.* E-rāsed', *blotted out.* 3. Pĕr'pe-trā-tor, *one who commits a crime.* Ex-tĭne'tion, *a putting an end to.* 4. Fĕr'ti-lize, *to make fruitful.* A'the-iṣm, *disbelief in God.* Sĕn-sū-ăl'i-ty, *indulgence in animal pleasure.*

XCIV. ROCK ME TO SLEEP.

Elizabeth Akers Allen (*b.* 1832, ———) was born at Strong, Maine, and passed her childhood amidst the picturesque scenery of that neighborhood. She lost her mother when very young, but inherited her grace and delicacy of thought. Shortly after her mother's death, her father removed to Farmington, Maine, a town noted for its literary people. Mrs. Allen's early pieces appeared over the pseudonym of "Florence Percy." Her first verses appeared when she was twelve years old; and her first volume, entitled "Forest Buds from the Woods of Maine," was published in 1856. For some years she was assistant-editor of the "Portland Transcript." The following selection was claimed by five different persons, who attempted to steal the honor of its composition.

1. BACKWARD, turn backward, O Time, in your flight,
    Make me a child again, just for to-night!
    Mother, come back from the echoless shore,
    Take me again to your heart as of yore;
    Kiss from my forehead the furrows of care,
    Smooth the few silver threads out of my hair;
    Over my slumbers your loving watch keep;—
    Rock me to sleep, mother,—rock me to sleep!

THE UNIVERSITY

Turning to higher education, what has become of our universities? Sadly, over the last half-century, many of the state universities of America have been infiltrated, subverted, and thoroughly transformed into intellectual cesspools advocating every imaginable left-wing, anti-Christian, anti-American, socialistic ideology. The universities have been hijacked and are now controlled by political and social liberalism. Many of the professors are atheistic, agnostic, and humanistic. They have been operating freely in order to make converts to their immoral, atheistic ideologies—from evolution to homosexuality. Indeed, the universities bear a large share of the blame for the silencing of God, dispelling belief in God, and jettisoning the Bible from among the last three generations of Americans.

But it was not always so. Indeed, from the very beginning of the nation—and before—the colleges were founded by ardent advocates of Christianity who designed these institutions of higher learning for a singular purpose: **to promote the Christian religion** among the inhabitants of America. Who can believe it? Such a claim sounds preposterous. Yet, the historical facts are plain and undeniable.

The first institution of higher education in the Colonies was Harvard College, founded in 1636. Named after its first benefactor, John Harvard, the 1636 rules of Harvard included the following declaration:

> Let every student be plainly instructed and earnestly pressed to consider well **the main end of his life and studies is to know God and Jesus Christ** which is eternal life (John 17.3) and therefore to lay Christ in the bottom as **the only foundation of all sound knowledge and learning**. And seeing the Lord only giveth wisdom,

let every one seriously set himself by prayer in secret to seek it of Him (Prov. 2,3). Every one shall so exercise himself in **reading the Scriptures twice a day** that he shall be ready to give such an account of his proficiency therein (as quoted in Pierce, 1833, p. 5, emp. added; parenthetical items in orig.).

John Harvard Statue at Harvard University, Cambridge, Massachusetts

The original seal of Harvard included the Latin word *veritas* which, according to the commencement remarks by the President of Harvard in 2002, meant "divine truth" and was "paired on the University's coat of arms with the University's real motto '*In Christi Gloriam*'" (Summers, 2002)—which means "For the Glory of Christ." Another motto that has been connected with the Harvard seal since the 1600s is *to et Ecclesiæ*— "For Christ and the Church" (Morison, p. 8).

Over a century after the founding of Harvard, the state [const]itution of Massachusetts reiterated the original and [conti]nuing purpose of the institution, which may still be seen [in th]e official Web site for the Commonwealth of Massachu-[setts.]Part the Second, Chapter V, Section 1 pertains to "THE [UNIV]ERSITY AT CAMBRIDGE, AND ENCOURAGEMENT OF [LITE]RATURE, ETC.":

Article I. Whereas our wise and pious ancestors, so early [a]s the year one thousand six hundred and thirty-six, laid [t]he foundation of Harvard College, in which university [m]any persons of great eminence have, **by the blessing of God**, been initiated in those arts and sciences, which qualified them for public employments, both **in church** [a]nd state: and whereas **the encouragement of arts and sciences, and all good literature, tends to the honor of God, the advantage of the Christian religion**, and [t]he great benefit of this and the other United States of America—it is declared, that the President and Fellows of Harvard College...shall have, hold, use, exercise and [e]njoy, all the powers...which they now have or are en-[t]itled to have (*Constitution of the Commonwealth*..., emp.

So according to the founders of Harvard, as well as the ar-chitects of the state constitution (themselves founders of the Republic), what was the purpose of education? To know God and Christ, to honor God, and to demonstrate the "advan-tage," i.e., superiority of, the Christian religion to the benefit of the entire country. Based on that original purpose, it is evident that education today is, to borrow a metaphor from Jesus, "like whitewashed tombs which indeed appear beauti-ful outwardly, but inside are full of dead men's bones and all uncleanness" (Matthew 23:27).

The founding of the other premiere institutions of high-er learning in America followed this same all-consuming, quintessential principle. For example, the second college established in America was William and Mary, founded in 1693. The charter, granted by the King and Queen of England, reads:

WILLIAM AND MARY, **by the grace of God**, of England, Scotland, France and Ireland, King and Queen, defend-ers of the Faith, &c. To all to whom these our present let-ters shall come, greeting. Forasmuch as our well-beloved and faithful subjects, constituting the General Assembly of our Colony of Virginia, have had it in their minds, and have proposed to themselves, **to the end that the Church of Virginia may be furnished with a seminary of ministers of the gospel**, and that the youth may be pi-ously educated in good letters and manners, and **that the Christian faith may be propagated amongst the West-ern Indians, to the glory of Almighty God**.... We, tak-ing the premises seriously into our consideration, and earnestly desiring, that as far as in us lies, true philoso-phy, and other good and liberal arts and sciences may be promoted, and **that the orthodox Christian faith may be propagated**...for promoting the studies of true philosophy, languages, and other good arts and scienc-es, and **for propagating the pure gospel of Christ, our**

God, may have power to erect, found and establish a certain place of universal study, or perpetual College, for Divinity, Philosophy, Languages and other good Arts and Sciences ("Royal Charter," emp. added).

First page of the Royal Charter of the College of William and Mary
Courtesy of Special Collections Research Center, Earl Gregg Swem Library, The College of William and Mary

In the 1758 volume, *The Charter, Transfer and Statutes of the College of William and Mary in Virginia*, the purpose for its founding was further explained:

> There are three things which the founders of this college proposed to themselves, to which all its statutes should be directed. The first is that the youth of Virginia should be well educated to learning **and good morals**. The second is that the churches of America, especially Virginia, should be **supplied with good ministers** after the doctrine and government of the Church of England, and that the college should be a constant seminary for this purpose. The third is that the Indians of America should be **instructed in the Christian religion**, and that some of the Indian youth that are well behaved and well inclined, being first well prepared in the Divinity School, may be sent out **to preach the gospel** to their countrymen in their own tongue (as quoted in Adler, 1968, 1:371, emp. added).

The third college established in America, Yale, was founded in 1701 and had as its stated purpose to be a school "wherein Youth may be instructed in the Arts and Sciences who **through the blessing of Almighty God** may be fitted for Publick employment **both in Church** and Civil State" ("About Yale," n.d.). The trustees stated the purpose on November 11, 1701 in the following words: "To plant, and under ye Divine blessing to propagate in this Wilderness, the blessed Reformed,

Old Campus building at Yale in New Haven, Connecticut

Protestant Religion, in ye purity of its Order, and Worship" (Mode, 1921, p. 109). They further stated: "Every student shall consider **the main end of his study** to wit **to know God in Jesus Christ and answerably to lead a Godly, sober life**" (Ringenberg, 1984, p. 38). Regulations for students at Yale in 1754 included strong religious requirements: "All scholars shall live religious, godly, and blameless lives according to the rules of God's Word, diligently reading the Holy Scriptures, the fountain of light and truth; and constantly attend upon all the duties of religion, both in public and secret" (as quoted in Adler, 1968, 1:464).

The fourth college established in America was Princeton, founded in 1746. In 1752, one of the trustees of the school, Gilbert Tennent, and Samuel Davies, later president, prepared a brochure describing the college, which included the following explanations of its intended purpose:

NOTHING has a more direct tendency to advance the happiness and glory of a community than the founding of public schools and seminaries of learning for education of youth, and adorning their minds with useful knowledge **and virtue**. Hereby, the rude and ignorant are civilized and rendered human; persons who would otherwise be useless members of society are qualified to sustain with honor the offices they may be invested with for the public service; **reverence of the Deity**, filial piety, and obedience to the laws are inculcated and promoted.... [S]everal gentlemen residing in and near the province of New Jersey, who were well-wishers to the felicity of their country and real friends of religion...first projected the scheme of a collegiate education in that province. **The immediate motives to this generous design were: the great number of Christian societies** then lately formed in various parts of the country, where many thousands of the inhabitants, **ardently desirous of the administra-**

tion of religious ordinances, were entirely destitute of the necessary means of instruction and incapable of being relieved.... the great scarcity of candidates **for the ministerial function to comply with these pious and Christian demands**.... [T]hese considerations were the most urgent arguments for the immediate prosecution of the above mentioned scheme of education.... It will suffice to say that the two principal objects the trustees had in view were science and **religion**. Their first concern was to cultivate the minds of the pupils in all those branches of erudition which are generally taught in the universities abroad; and, **to perfect their design, their next care was to rectify the heart by inculcating the great precepts of Christianity in order to make them good**. Upon these views this society was founded.... But as **religion ought to be the end of all instruction** and gives it the last degree of perfection...[s]tated times are set apart for **the study of the Holy Scriptures** in the original languages, and stated hours daily consecrated to the service of religion. The utmost care is taken to discountenance vice and to encourage the practice of virtue and a manly, rational, and **Christian** behavior in the students (Davies and Tennent, 1754, emp. added).

Old Campus building at Princeton University in Princeton, New Jersey

Dartmouth was founded in 1769 by "Reverend Eleazar Wheelock" by a charter granted by King George III to spread Christianity—initially to Indian youths:

KNOW YE, THEREFORE that We, considering the premises and being willing to encourage the laudable and charitable design of **spreading Christian knowledge** among the savages of our American wilderness, and also that the best means of education be established in our province of New Hampshire, for the benefit of said province, do, of our special grace, certain knowledge and mere motion, by and with the advice of our counsel for said province, by these presents, will, ordain, grant and constitute that there be a college erected in our said province of New Hampshire by the name of Dartmouth College, for the education and instruction of youth of the Indian tribes in this land in reading, writing, and all parts of learning which shall appear necessary and expedient for civilizing **and christianizing** children of pagans, as well as in all liberal arts and sciences, and also of English youth and any others. And the trustees of said college may and shall be one body corporate and politic, in deed, action and name, and shall be called, named and distinguished by the name of the Trustees of Dartmouth College (*Charter of Dartmouth...*, emp. added).

Harvard, William and Mary, Yale, Princeton, Dartmouth—this listing could be significantly expanded.

Even a brief glance at some of the original school mottos testifies to the purpose of education in America from the beginning (see "List of...," n.d.). For example, Brown University, the seventh oldest institution of higher learning in the United States, founded by Baptist preachers in 1764 as Rhode Island College, has the motto *In deo speramus*, Latin for "In God We Hope." Princeton's motto is *Dei sub numine viget*, meaning "Under the Protection of God She Flourishes." On the Princeton University shield is an open book inscribed with *Vet. Nov. Testamentum* which means "Old and New Testament." Dartmouth's motto is *Vox clamantis in deserto*, translated "A Voice Crying in the Wilderness," a reference to Isaiah's prophecy of John the Baptizer in Isaiah 40:3 (cf. Matthew 3:3). Another Ivy League school, founded in 1754 as King's College, renamed Columbia College when it reopened in 1784 after the American Revolution, and now Columbia University, has the motto *In lumine Tuo videbimus lumen*, which means "In Thy Light Shall We See Light."

Woodcut of the Founding of Dartmouth, 1769.
Courtesy of Dartmouth College Library

Brown University Seal

The Old Princeton Shield
© Princeton University

George Washington University was chartered in 1821 (on land provided by George Washington) as Columbian College with the motto *Deus Nobis Fiducia*—"In God Our Trust." The university Web site describes the university seal as including "an open Testament showing the following words in Greek from Chapter I, verses 1-4, of the Gospel according to St. John, on the left page: 'In the beginning was the Word, and the Word was with God, and the Word was God,' and, on the right page: 'In Him was life, and the life was the light of men'" ("University Seal," 2002).

Northwestern University was founded in 1851 by Methodists from Chicago to serve Americans in the Northwest Territory. The motto on Northwestern's seal is *Quaecumque sunt vera*, meaning "Whatsoever things are true"—taken from Philippians 4:8. Also on the seal is a Greek phrase inscribed on the pages of an open book: *ho logos pleres charitos kai aletheias,* which translates as "The Word...full of grace and truth"—a reference to Jesus Christ taken from John 1:14. Even the University of California at Berkeley, a school known for its student activism, rebellion against America's Christian heritage, and its "hippie" counterculture in the 1960s, has a Bible-inspired motto, "Let There Be Light," taken from Genesis 1:3.

Courtesy of Northwestern University

The University of California's Seal

The American educational system has strayed far from its moorings. We have shifted from a nation that saw **its very survival as dependent on the spread of Christian principles through the schools,** to a nation that literally disdains, repudiates, and has ejected the teaching of Christian principles from the educational system. The Founders would be appalled. Physician and signer of the *Declaration of Independence*, Dr. Benjamin Rush, asserted: "[T]he only foundation for a useful education in a republic is to be laid **in religion**. Without this there can be **no virtue**, and without virtue there can be **no liberty**, and liberty is the object and life of all republican governments" (1798, p. 8, emp. added). Dr. Rush further stated:

> We profess to be republicans, and yet we neglect the only means of establishing and perpetuating our republican forms of government, that is, **the universal education of our youth in the principles of Christianity by the means of the Bible**. For this Divine Book, above all others, favors that equality among mankind, that respect for just laws, and those sober and frugal virtues, which constitute the soul of republicanism (pp. 93-94, emp. added).

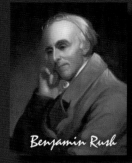

Benjamin Rush

Noah Webster echoed those sentiments: "In my view, **the Christian religion is the most important** and one of the first things in which all children, under a free government, ought to be instructed" (1843, p. 291, emp. added). The words of God to Moses at Mt. Sinai ought to serve as the guiding star for America's schools: "Gather the people to Me, and I will let them hear My words, that they may learn to fear Me all the days they live on the earth, and that they may teach their children" (Deuteronomy 4:10). "Come, you children, listen to me; I will teach you the fear of the Lord" (Psalm 34:11). Without the fear of the Lord instilled in the nation's youth, **all will be lost** (Deuteronomy 5:33; 6:1-18; Jeremiah 7:23).

MISCELLANEOUS MANIFESTA-TIONS OF GOD IN PUBLIC LIFE

THE PONY EXPRESS

Pony Express Bible, 1858

Other indications of the Christian religion characterizing public life in America thoroughly permeate history. For example, many Americans are aware of the famed Pony Express—a novel mail service that operated from April, 1860 to November, 1861, enabling letters sent from St. Joseph, Missouri to arrive in San Francisco in a phenomenal 10 days (as opposed to months later). But few know that **every Pony Express rider was required to carry in his saddle bags a copy of the Bible** ("The Bible," n.d.)! Each rider was also required to take the following oath:

I, ____, do hereby swear, before **the Great and Living God**, that during my engagement, and while I am an employee of Russell, Majors and Waddell, I will, under no circumstances, use profane language, that I will drink no intoxicating liquors, that I will not quarrel or fight with any other employee of the firm, and that in every respect I will conduct myself honestly, be faithful to my duties, and so direct all my acts as to win the confidence of my employers, **so help me God** ("Pony Express History," n.d., emp. added).

Images courtesy of Bancroft Library, UC Berkeley

MOTEL BIBLES, BLUE LAWS, HIGHWAY CROSSES, CITY NAMES

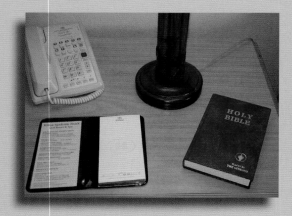

What about the fact that a Bible (provided by the Gideons—see "History of the Association," n.d.) is located in virtually every hotel and motel room in the country? Not a Quran or the Buddhist Patakis. Further, consider the so-called "Blue laws" that were in force nation-wide from before the beginning of the nation in which most businesses were required to close on Sunday in observance of the day of Christian worship ("Blue law," 2008). Yet, these, too, since the 1960s, have been nearly expunged by the systematic silencing of God in recent years (Miller, "In Battle for...," 2003). What about the placement of crosses on the nation's highways commemorating those who have died in automobile accidents? What about the myriad of names for geographical locations across the country that have come straight from the Bible? Everything from Bethlehem (in 19 states!) and Antioch (in 20 states) to Corpus Christi (Body of Christ), Texas and Las Cruces (The Crosses), New Mexico. All names that begin with San (San Francisco, San Antonio, San Diego, etc.) or Santa (Santa Fe [Holy Faith], Santa Monica, Santa Anita, etc.) are of Christian derivation.

CEMETERIES

What will the ACLU do about our cemeteries, in which graves are frequently marked with crosses and words from the Bible? Even our military (i.e, government) cemeteries are characterized by their connection to the Christian religion. In fact, in our military cemeteries in foreign lands (eight World War I and 14 World War II), with the occasional exception of a star of David, each constitutes a visually stunning sea of white, marble crosses ("Cemeteries"). The allusions to the Bible and the Christian religion permeate the cemeteries throughout America.

Aisne-Marne
Belleau, France

Meuse-Argonne
Romagne-sous-Montfaucon, France

Somme
Bony, France

Brookwood
Brookwood, Surrey, England

Oise-Aisne
Fère-en-Tardenois, France

St. Mihiel
Thiaucourt, France

Flanders Field
Waregem, Belgium

Chapel at Suresnes

GRANT UNTO THEM O LORD ETERNAL REST
WHO SLEEP IN UNKNOWN GRAVES

Suresnes
Suresnes, France

World War I cemeteries
Courtesy of the American Battle Monuments Commission, Arlington, Virginia

Ardennes
Neupré, Belgium

Brittany
St. James, France

Cambridge
Cambridge, England

Florence
Florence, Italy

Rhone
Draguignan, France

Epinal
Epinal, France

Henri-Chapelle
Henri-Chapelle, Belgium

Lorraine
St. Avold, France

Manila
Global City, Philippines

World War II cemeteries
Courtesy of the American Battle Monuments Commission, Arlington, Virginia

Luxembourg
Hamm, Luxembourg

Chapel at Luxembourg
with cross and John 10:28

Netherlands
Margraten, Netherlands

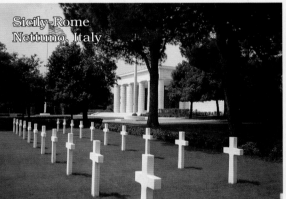

Sicily-Rome
Nettuno, Italy

North Africa
Carthage, Tunisia

Normandy with Omaha Beach
and the English Channel below

World War II cemeteries
Courtesy of the American Battle Monuments Commission, Arlington, Virginia

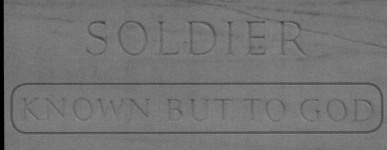

Tomb of the Unknown Soldier, Arlington National Cemetery

SUMMARY

S uch manifestations of America's intimate affiliation with the God of the Bible and the Christian religion are legion. They could be multiplied many times over. Indeed, the evidence for America's Christian heritage is massive, expansive, and decisive. The conspiracy to remove them is in direct contradiction to over 185+ years of **proof** to the contrary. From the very beginning of the country, and extending for over a century and a half, this nation claimed that the God of the Bible was the God of America. The Founders did not seek freedom **from** religion, but freedom **for** religion—specifically, the **Christian** religion. But in just 50 years, subversive forces have been working overtime to expel God from culture and American civilization. They have accomplished so much that the America of the 21ˢᵗ century is in many respects a **different country** from the America of the 18ᵗʰ, 19ᵗʰ, and 20ᵗʰ centuries. How so? Read carefully the words of Alexis de Tocqueville, French historian and politician, who visited America in 1831 and 1832, traveling the country and surveying American life. Upon his return to France, he penned his monumental *Democracy in America* (1835), which included the following astounding observations:

Alexis de Tocqueville

[T]here is no country in the world where **the Christian religion retains a greater influence over the souls of men than in America**; and there can be no greater proof of its utility and of its conformity to human nature than that **its influence is powerfully felt over the most enlightened and free nation of the earth**.... Christianity, therefore, reigns without obstacle, by universal consent; the consequence is, as I have before observed, that **every principle of the moral world is fixed** and determinate.... [T]he revolutionists of America are obliged to profess an ostensible **respect for Christian morality** and equity, which does not permit them to violate wantonly the laws that oppose their designs.... [W]hile the law permits the Americans to do what they please, **religion prevents them** from conceiving, and forbids them to commit, what is rash or unjust.... I do not know whether all Americans have a sincere faith in **their religion**—for who can search the human heart?—but I am certain that **they hold it to be indispensable to the maintenance of republican institutions**. This opinion is not peculiar to a class of citizens or to a party, but **it belongs to the whole nation and to every rank of society**.... The Americans **combine the notions of Christianity and of liberty** so intimately in their minds that it is impossible to make them conceive the one without the other.... **How is it possible that society should escape destruction if the moral tie is not strengthened in proportion as the political tie is relaxed?** And what can be done with a people who are their own masters **if they are not submissive to the Deity**? (1835, 1:303-307, emp. added).

Haunting questions, indeed. Sadly, the America of which he spoke in 1835 is not the America of today.

WHAT CAN BE DONE?

If Christians do not rise up and act, the downward spiral will continue, eventually resulting in inevitable catastrophe. So what may be done? What would God have Christians to do? "If the foundations are destroyed, what can the righteous do?" (Psalm 11:3). Consider the following succinct listing of seven recommended actions that could turn the nation around if enacted by a sizable number of Americans:

I. Self-examination and rededication of one's own life to serious devotion to God, Christ, and the moral principles on which the Republic was founded.

II. Diligent dedication of one's own family to God and Christ. Consider homeschooling to shield children from the subversion of political correctness that has enshrouded public schools. Return to modeling the home according to the Bible's directives, including:

> And these words which I command you today shall be in your heart. You shall teach them diligently to your children, and shall talk of them when you sit in your house, when you walk by the way, when you lie down, and when you rise up (Deuteronomy 6:6-7).

> Fathers, do not exasperate your children; instead, bring them up in the training and instruction of the Lord (Ephesians 6:4). Wives, submit to your husbands, as is fitting in the Lord. Husbands, love your wives and do not be harsh with them. Children, obey your parents in everything, for this pleases the Lord. Fathers, do not embitter your children, or they will become discouraged (Colossians 3:18-21, NIV).

> He who spares his rod hates his son, but he who loves him disciplines him promptly. Chasten your son while there is hope, and do not set your heart on his destruction. Foolishness is bound up in the heart of a child; the rod of correction will drive it far from him. Do not withhold correction from a child, for if you beat him with a rod, he will not die. You shall beat him with a rod, and deliver his soul from hell. The rod and rebuke give wisdom, but a child left to himself brings shame to his mother. Correct your son, and he will give you rest; yes, he will give delight to your soul (Proverbs 13:24; 19:18; 22:15; 23:13-14; 29:15,17).

...d. In fact, during the seven years of the Revolutionary War, the Continental Congress issued no fewer than nine public ...ions to the American people, calling upon the whole nation to set aside entire days in which no labor would be perfo... ...t the citizens could devote themselves to praying to God (Miller, 2006a).

In CONGRESS,
NOVEMBER 1, 1777.

FORASMUCH as it is the indispensible duty of all men to adore the superintending providence of Almighty God; to acknowledge with gratitude their obligations to HIM for benefits received; and to implore such farther blessings as they stand in need of: And it having pleased him in his abundant mercy, not only to continue to us the *innumerable* bounties of his common providence; but also to smile upon us, in the prosecution of a just and necessary war for the defence and establishment of our unalienable rights and liberties: *Particularly* in that he hath been pleased in so great a measure, to prosper the means used for the support of our troops, and to crown our arms with most *signal* success:

It is therefore recommended to the legislative or executive powers of these United States, to set apart THURSDAY, the eighteenth day of December next, for SOLEMN THANKSGIVING and PRAISE: That at one time and with one voice, the good people may express the grateful feelings of their hearts, and consecrate themselves to the service of their DIVINE BENEFACTOR: and that, together with their sincere acknowledgments and offerings, they may join the penitent confession of their sins, whereby they had forfeited every favor; and their humble and earnest supplications that it may please God through the merits of *Jesus Christ*, mercifully to forgive and *blot* them out of remembrance. That it may please him graciously to afford his blessing on the Governments of these States respectively, and prosper the PUBLIC COUNCIL of the whole. To inspire our commanders both by land and sea, and all under them, with that wisdom and fortitude which may render them fit instruments, under the providence of Almighty God, to secure for these United States, the greatest of all human blessings, INDEPENDENCE and PEACE. That it may please him, to prosper the trade and manufactures of the people, and the labour of the husbandman, that our land may yet yield its increase. To take schools and seminaries of education, so necessary for cultivating the principles of true liberty, virtue and piety, under his *nurturing* hand: and to prosper the means of religion, for the promotion and enlargement of that kingdom which consisteth "IN RIGHTEOUSNESS, PEACE AND JOY IN THE HOLY GHOST."

And it is further recommended, that servile labour, and such recreation as, though at other times innocent, may be unbecoming the purpose of this appointment, may be omitted on so solemn an occasion.

By order of CONGRESS.

HENRY LAURENS, President.

STATE OF MASSACHUSETTS-BAY.
COUNCIL-CHAMBER, in BOSTON, *November 27, 1777.*

AGREEABLE to the above recommendation of the honorable CONTINENTAL CONGRESS, by the advice of the COUNCIL, and at the desire of the HOUSE of REPRESENTATIVES, we have thought fit to appoint, and do hereby appoint THURSDAY the eighteenth day of December next, to be observed throughout this State as a day of public THANKSGIVING and PRAISE: And we do hereby call upon Ministers and People of every denomination, religiously to observe the said day accordingly.

Jeremiah Powell,
Artemas Ward,
Walter Spooner,
Richard Derby, Junr.
Thomas Cushing,
Samuel Holton,
Jabez Fisher,
Moses Gill,
John Taylor,
Benjamin White,
Benjamin Austin,
Daniel Davis,
Daniel Hopkins,
Nathan Cushing,
Abraham Fuller.

By their Honor's Command,

JOHN AVERY, Dep. Sec'ry.

GOD SAVE THE UNITED STATES of AMERICA!

PROCLAMATION.

THE Goodness of the supreme Being to all his rational Creatures, demands their Acknowledgements of Gratitude and Love; his absolute Government of the World dictates, that it is the Interest of every Nation and People ardently to supplicate his Favour and implore his Protection.

When the Lust of Dominion or lawless Ambition excites arbitrary Power to invade the Rights, or endeavour to wrest from a People their sacred and invaluable Privileges, and compels them, in Defence of the same, to encounter all the Horrors and Calamities of a bloody and vindictive War; then is that People loudly called upon to fly unto that God for Protection, who hears the Cries of the distressed, and will not turn a deaf Ear to the Supplication of the oppressed.

Great-Britain, hitherto, left to infatuated Councils, and to pursue Measures repugnant to her own Interest and distressing to this Country, still persists in the Design of subjugating these United States; which will compel us into another active and perhaps bloody Campaign.

The United States in Congress assembled, therefore, taking into Consideration our present Situation, our multiplied Transgressions of the holy Laws of our God, and his past Acts of Kindness and Goodness towards us, which we ought to record with the liveliest Gratitude, think it their indispensible Duty to call upon the several States, to set apart the last *Thursday* in *April* next, as a Day of *Fasting, Humiliation,* and *Prayer*; that our joint Supplications may then ascend to the Throne of the Ruler of the Universe, beseeching him to diffuse a Spirit of universal Reformation among all Ranks and Degrees of our Citizens, and make us a holy, that so we be an happy People; that it would please him to impart Wisdom, Integrity, and Unanimity to our Counsellors; to bless and prosper the Reign of our illustrious Ally, and give Success to his Arms employed in the Defence of the Rights of human Nature; that he would smile upon our military Arrangements by Land and Sea; administer Comfort and Consolation to our Prisoners in a cruel Captivity; protect the Health and Life of our Commander in Chief; grant us Victory over our Enemies; establish Peace in all our Borders, and give Happiness to all our Inhabitants; that he would prosper the Labour of the Husbandman, making the Earth yield its encrease in Abundance, and give a proper Season for the ingathering of the Fruits thereof; that he would grant Success to all engaged in lawful Trade and Commerce, and take under his Guardianship all Schools and Seminaries of Learning, and make them Nurseries of Virtue and Piety; that he would incline the Hearts of all Men to Peace, and fill them with universal Charity and Benevolence, and that the Religion of our Divine Redeemer, with all its benign Influences, may cover the Earth as the Waters cover the Seas.

DONE by the United States in Congress assembled, this nineteenth Day of March, in the Year of Lord One Thousand seven Hundred and eighty two, and in the sixth Year of our Independence.

JOHN HANSON, President.

Attest. CHARLES THOMSON, Sec'ry.

By His EXCELLENCY,
JONATHAN TRUMBULL, Esquire,
Governor, and Commander in Chief in and over the State of *Connecticut*, in *America*.

PROCLAMATION.

ON Consideration of, and in chearful compliance with the foregoing Call of Congress on all the United States,

I HAVE thought fit, by and with Advice of Council, to appoint, and do hereby appoint, the last *Thursday* of *April* Instant, as a Day of *Fasting, Humiliation* and *Prayer*; requiring and exhorting all Orders and Denominations of People within this State, to set apart and solemnize the same; to offer joint Supplications to Almighty God, agreeably to the Proclamation of the United States in Congress assembled.

All servile Labour is forbidden on said Day.

GIVEN under my Hand at Lebanon, this tenth Day of April, in the Year of our Lord one thousand seven hundred and eighty two, and in the sixth Year of the Independence of the United States of America.

JONATH. TRUMBULL.

NEW-LONDON: Printed by TIMOTHY GREEN, Printer to the Governor and Company.

Left: November 1, 1777 Continental Congress Proclamation. Right: March 19, 1782 Continental Congress Proclamation.

The Founders were merely echoing the Bible's own teaching regarding the necessity of petitioning God for national assistance and protection:

Therefore I exhort first of all that supplications, prayers, intercessions, and giving of thanks be made for all men, for kings and all who are in authority, that we may lead a quiet and peaceable life in all godliness and reverence (1 Timothy 2:1-2).

And shall God not avenge His own elect who **cry out day and night to Him**, though He bears long with them? I tell you that He will avenge them speedily (Luke 18:7-8, emp. added).

However, keep in mind that a sufficient number of Americans may have so rejected God that He intends to punish America. The Founders were poignantly aware of this very possibility, as expressed by them in a proclamation they released to the American public on March 20, 1779: "Whereas, in just punishment of our manifold transgressions, it hath pleased the Supreme Disposer of all events to visit these United States with a destructive calamitous war" (*Journals of...*, 1909, 13:343-344).

The time has come to face the fact that America may have plummeted too far in its departure from God's will to be recalled. Young King Josiah came to this very realization when, having discovered the Book of the Law which had been lost amid temple debris, its precepts largely neglected by the nation, in panic he announced: "[G]reat is the wrath of the Lord that is aroused against us, because our fathers have not obeyed the words of this book, to do according to all that is written concerning us" (2 Kings 22:13). Though God was pleased with Josiah's humility and tender heart, disaster was inevitable:

Thus says the Lord: "Behold, I will bring calamity on this place and on its inhabitants...because they have forsaken Me.... Therefore My wrath shall be aroused against this place and shall not be quenched" (2 Kings 22:16-17).

If this be the precise predicament of America, we ought humbly to embrace the attitude of the psalmist when he said:

O Lord God, to whom vengeance belongs—O God, to whom vengeance belongs, shine forth! **Rise up, O Judge of the earth; render punishment to the proud**. Lord, how long will the wicked, how long will the wicked triumph?... Understand, you senseless among the people; and you fools, when will you be wise? He who planted the ear, shall He not hear? He who formed the eye, shall He not see? He who instructs the nations, **shall He not correct**, He who teaches man knowledge? The Lord knows the thoughts of man, that they are futile (Psalm 94:1-3,8-11, emp. added).

The nations have sunk down in the pit which they made; in the net which they hid, their own foot is caught. The Lord is known by the judgment He executes; the wicked is snared in the work of his own hands. The wicked shall be turned into hell, and **all the nations that forget God**.... Arise, O Lord, do not let man prevail; **let the nations be judged** in Your sight. Put them in fear, O Lord, **that the nations may know themselves to be but men** (Psalm 9:15-20, emp. added).

When we plead with God on behalf of the nation, our every petition must be tempered with the same resignation Jesus manifested in the Garden: "O My Father, if it is possible, let this cup pass from Me; nevertheless, **not as I will, but as You will**" (Matthew 26:39, emp. added; cf. James 4:15).

IV. Learn the Bible—deeply and thoroughly. Delve into God's Word. Show respect for His thinking by pouring over its contents. Encourage family and friends to do the same. The Founders viewed the Bible as absolutely indispensable and integral to the survival of the Republic, citing it in their political utterances far more often than any other source (see Lutz, 1988, pp. 140-141). Indeed, consider the eloquent testimony to this fact, as expressed by a few of the Founders. For example, *Constitution* signer and Secretary of War, James McHenry, insisted:

> The Holy Scriptures...can **alone** secure to society, order and peace, and to our courts of justice and constitutions of government, purity, stability, and usefulness. In vain, **without the Bible**, we increase penal laws and draw entrenchments around our institutions. **Bibles are strong entrenchments. Where they abound, men cannot pursue wicked courses** (Steiner, 1921, p. 14, emp. added).

Patrick Henry believed that the Bible "is a book worth more than all the other books that were ever printed" (as quoted in Wirt, 1818, p. 402). John Jay wrote to Peter Jay on April 8, 1784: "The Bible is the best of all books, for it is the word of God and teaches us the way to be happy in this world and in the next" (1980, 2:709). Noah Webster asserted: "The Bible is the chief moral cause of all that is good and the best corrector of all that is evil in human society; the best book for regulating the temporal concerns of men" (1833, p. v). He further claimed: "All the miseries and evils which men suffer from vice, crime, ambition, injustice, oppression, slavery and war, proceed from their despising or neglecting the precepts contained in the Bible" (1832, p. 339). *Constitution* signer, Gouverneur Morris, observed: "The reflection and experience of many years have led me to consider the holy writings not only as the most authentic and instructive in themselves, but as the clue to all other history. They tell us what man is, and they alone tell us why he is what he is" (1821, p. 30). *Declaration* signer, Dr. Benjamin Rush, declared that the Bible "should be read in our schools in preference to all other books from its containing the greatest portion of that kind of knowledge which is calculated to produce private and public temporal happiness" (1798, p. 100). In a letter to Thomas Jefferson on December 25, 1813, John Adams stated that "the Bible is the best Book in the world" (1856, 10:85).

Indeed, Americans need a strong dose of the absolutely critical essentiality of the Bible to both national and private life, as stated by the Bible writers themselves:

> I will never forget Your precepts, **for by them You have given me life**. Oh, how I love Your law! It is my meditation all the day. You, through Your commandments, **make me wiser than my enemies**; for they are ever with me. I understand more than the ancients, because I keep Your precepts. How sweet are Your words to my taste, sweeter than honey to my mouth! Through Your precepts **I get under-**

standing; **therefore I hate every false way**. Your word is a lamp to my feet and a light to my path (Psalm 119:93,97-98,100,103-105, emp. added).

For **the word of God is living and powerful**, and sharper than any two-edged sword, piercing even to the division of soul and spirit, and of joints and marrow, and is **a discerner of the thoughts and intents of the heart** (Hebrews 4:12, emp. added).

If you **abide in My word**, you are My disciples indeed. And you shall know the truth, and **the truth shall make you free**.... He who rejects Me, and does not receive My words, has that which judges him— **the word that I have spoken will judge him in the last day**.... Sanctify them by Your truth. **Your word is truth** (John 8:31-32; 12:48; 17:17, emp. added).

The future of the Republic is inextricably linked with and inherently dependent on the extent to which Americans are willing to return to an intimate acquaintance with the Bible.

V. Petition politicians, school board members, and the media regarding **spiritual** (not political) issues, focusing simply and solely on **morality**—not money. Think about it: Here is the real gist of this book. Here is what this entire subject comes down to. As one steps back and evaluates the moral and spiritual condition of America, it is self-evident that our nation has strayed far from its moorings just in the last half-century. America is now unquestionably characterized by rampant divorce, widespread sexual impurity, gambling, drunkenness, thievery, and the list goes on. Prisons are full to overflowing with more being built as swiftly as possible, in conjunction with early release programs. Crime statistics are at an all-time high in virtually every category. While sin (i.e., violations of God's will—1 John 3:4) has increased in the land, **two sins stand out from all others in our day**. Two sins, par-

ticularly repugnant in God's sight, have swept over America. These two sins have been **politicized**—instead of being left in the moral and religious arena where they belong. These two premiere moral issues facing the country are **abortion** and **homosexuality**. A nation can survive for a period of time even when murder, theft, adultery, and the like are rampant. (After all, sin is sin. All sin is destructive and eventually will be addressed by a perfect God.) However, history shows that when some sins become pervasive in a given civilization, its demise is imminent. The killing of children and sexual perversion are just such sins. Ultimately, America's drifting from its spiritual moorings is climaxing in imminent moral implosion and inevitable retribution from God based on these two critical moral matters. Please consider them briefly.

ABORTION

Who could have imagined (the Founders most certainly could not have done so) that America would ever give legal sanction to a woman to kill her unborn baby? Yet, the 1973 U.S. Supreme Court did just that by ruling that "the word 'person' as used in the Fourteenth Amendment, does not include the unborn" (*Roe v. Wade*). Who could have imagined one day that more than 48 million babies would be butchered in the United States of America? And that figure does not include the millions more being sacrificed in the name of embryonic "stem-cell research," as well as the millions more lost from selective reduction due to the use of fertility drugs. The killing of the innocent (Exodus 23:7), and the shedding of innocent blood—a thing that God hates (Proverbs 6)—are widespread in the land. If the voice of Abel's blood cried out to God from the soil on which his brother had shed it

(Genesis 4:10), the blood of millions of babies shrieking and screaming to God must be absolutely deafening.

If you care what God thinks, I urge you to read Exodus 21:22-25, Ecclesiastes 11:5, Psalm 139:13-16, Isaiah 49:1, Jeremiah 1:4-5, Zechariah 12:1, and Galatians 1:15. Read the three phases of human life in Hosea 9:11—conception, pregnancy, and birth. Read where God used the same Greek word (*brephos*) to refer to John in his mother's womb that He used to refer to the baby Jesus lying in the manger (Luke 1:39-45; 2:12,16), as well as the use of "son" to refer to John *in utero* (Luke 1:36). Read what is essentially an ancient description of the heinous practice of partial-birth abortion in Exodus 1:15-22. Read about God's outrage at the Israelites for sacrificing their children to pagan deities—a reprehensible act that never entered God's mind to enjoin (Jeremiah 19:5; 32:35). The Bible clearly teaches that God possesses personal regard for human life from the moment of conception.

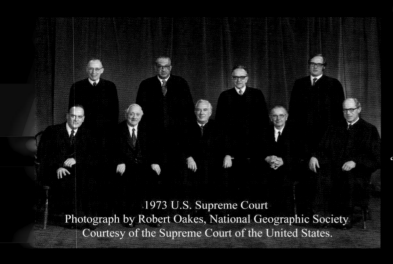

1973 U.S. Supreme Court
Photograph by Robert Oakes, National Geographic Society
Courtesy of the Supreme Court of the United States.

Our own medical science verifies the same thing. Samuel Armas was a 21-week unborn baby when doctors at Vanderbilt University Medical Center in Nashville, Tennessee performed spina bifida surgery on him while he was still in his mother's womb. During the surgery, his little hand flopped out of the incision opening and rested on the doctor's fingers. Eyewitness photo journalist Michael Clancy insists that Samuel's fingers gripped the doctor's finger (see Clancy, 2001). In any case, Samuel was born 15 weeks later. There was nothing about his exit from his mother's body that suddenly transformed him from a nonhuman into a human. He was a human throughout his pre-birth circumstance (see Lyons, 2007; Imbody, 2003; Solenni, 2003).

A terrible and tragic inconsistency and incongruity exists in America. Merely taking possession of an egg containing the pre-born American bald eagle—let alone if one were to destroy that little pre-birth environment and thus destroy the baby eagle that is developing within—results in a stiff fine and even prison time. Yet one can take a human child in its pre-born environment and not only murder that child, but also receive government blessing to do so! Eagle eggs, i.e., pre-born eagles, are of greater value to American civilization than pre-born humans (see Miller, 2004)! What has happened to our society? This state of affairs cannot be harmonized in a consistent, rational fashion. The ethics and moral sensibilities that underlie this circumstance are absolutely bizarre (Miller, "Abortion...," 2003).

The number of known abortions in America since 1973 is nearing 50 million—approximately 50 times more than all Americans lost in all of our wars. That figure is staggering, if not incomprehensible, to the human mind. That figure constitutes essentially one-sixth of the present U.S. population. If we awoke in the morning to face the terrifying news that terrorists had detonated nuclear devices in major urban areas that resulted in the death of 50 million Americans, we would be shocked, panic-stricken, and heartsick. Or imagine a deadly virus released by unconscionable terrorists that wiped out the populations of the following red states:

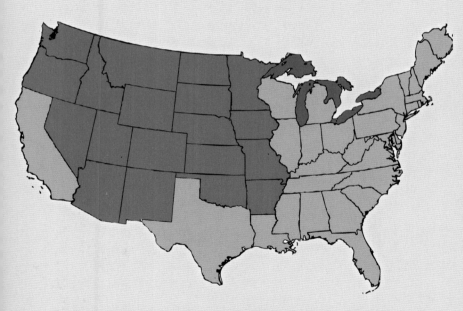

The combined population of the above red states is equivalent to the number of reported abortions in America since 1973.

Yet, Americans have tolerated the execution of that many of its children—entire generations of young people who will never see the light of day. I wonder if one of those would have found the cure for cancer. What untold potential and productivity has been snuffed out by a calloused, cruel, self-centered people! At least the pagans of antiquity killed their children for **religious** purposes, thinking they were pleasing a higher authority. We do it mostly for **convenience**—to evade the consequences of the sexual anarchy that runs rampant across our civilization.

The ethical disharmony and moral confusion that reign in our society have escalated the activity of criminals who commit a variety of heinous crimes—from murdering and maiming fellow-citizens on a daily basis, to raping women and molesting children. Yet, a sizeable portion of society is against capital punishment. Many people feel that these wicked adults, who have engaged in heinous, destructive conduct, should not be executed (a viewpoint that flies directly in the face of what the Founders believed and what the Bible teaches [Romans 13:1-6; 1 Peter 2:13-14], since God wants evildoers in society to be punished—even to the point of capital punishment). So we rarely execute guilty, hardened criminals. **But we daily execute innocent human babies!** How can one possibly accept this terrible disparity, the horrible scourge of abortion?

The latest polls verify our deteriorating morality. An *ABC News/Washington Post* Poll conducted in June of 2008 reveals that 53% of adult Americans believe that abortion should be legal in all or most cases, while a May 2008 Gallup poll found that 82% believe that abortion should be legal under any or certain circumstances, with only 17% maintaining that abortion should be illegal under all circumstances (see "Abortion and Birth Control").

The nation has embraced moral insanity. Abortion is a glaring manifestation of the expulsion of God from American culture. Mark it down: *THE GOD OF THE BIBLE WILL NOT ALLOW THIS MONSTROUS ATROCITY TO GO UNCHALLENGED AND UNPUNISHED.*

HOMOSEXUALITY

As if killing the unborn were not enough to condemn a civilization to eternal punishment, America is experiencing another horror of seismic proportions. Charles Haynes, a senior scholar at the First Amendment Center in Arlington, Virginia, commented on the issue of gay rights in the face of a nationwide contest over religious and civil rights: "Everyone's talking about it, thinking about it. There are a lot of different ideas about where we are going to end up, but **everyone thinks it is the battle of our times**" (as quoted in Gallagher, 11[33], 2006; cf. Haynes, 2006). A sobering realization. Think of it: *the battle of our times.* Of those living today in America who were alive 50 years ago, few could have imagined, let alone predicted, that homosexuality would encroach on our culture as it has. In fact, it would have been unthinkable. The rapidity with which homosexual activists continue successfully to bully the nation to normalize what once was universally considered abnormal is astonishing. And toleration has not satisfied them. Allowing their views to be taught in public schools has not appeased them. No, they insist that societal endorsement extend to redefining marriage to include same-sex couples.

A pernicious plague of sexual insanity is creeping insidiously through American civilization. Far more deadly than the external threat of terrorism, or even the inevitable dilution of traditional American values caused by the infiltration of illegal immigrants and the influx of those who do not share the Christian worldview, this domino effect will ultimately end in the moral implosion of America. Indeed, America is being held captive by moral terrorists. The social engineers of "political correctness" have been working overtime for decades to restructure public morality. In 1973, the American Psychiatric Association deleted homosexuality from its official nomenclature of mental disorders, the *Diagnostic and Statistical Manual of Mental Disorders* (DSM), and the American Psychological Association followed suit in 1975 (see "Gay and Lesbian...," 2002; Herek, 2002). Large corporations and businesses across the country have been subjecting their employees to mass propaganda under the guise of "sensitivity training."

Among those who are attempting to coerce the country into altering its long-standing code of Christian moral values are activist judges. Their tortured "interpretation" of constitutional law demonstrates that they have no respect for God, existing laws, America's history, or the will of the people. Instead, they apparently see themselves as qualified social architects to redefine marriage and morality by usurping their constitutional role and legislating from the bench. They have placed themselves at odds with the history of Western civilization. With no regard for American legal history and the body of constitutional law that has remained largely intact from the beginning of the nation until the mid-20th century, they essentially have brushed aside over 150 years of American judicial history with a flippant wave of the hand. They are literally restructuring the American moral landscape with an unflinching vengeance that is undaunted by the widespread national outrage to the contrary. Those who characterized governmental control and Christian morality in the 1960s as equivalent to Orwell's "Big Brother" are now living a self-fulfilled prophecy—they **are** "Big Brother."

These judicial junkies are aided by politicians from the left coast to the east coast, who have taken it upon themselves to issue marriage licenses for homosexual partners. Additionally, the public school system is being transformed into an incubator for nurturing the next generation of Americans, breaking down any resistance they might otherwise have had toward the impropriety of homosexuality. These developments were inevitable in the wake of the U.S. Supreme Court's historically and constitutionally unprecedented elimination of state sodomy laws (*Lawrence...*, 2003). The high court's decision was a reversal of its 1986 decision that upheld State sodomy laws and reinforced the historic stance that homosexuality is **not a constitutional right** (see *Bowers...*). What's more, no bona fide scientific evidence exists to demonstrate any genetic cause of homosexuality—even as no genuine genetic linkage will ever be forthcoming to legitimize pedophilia, bestiality, polygamy, or incest (see Harrub and Miller, 2004, 24[8]:73-79). Indeed, homosexuality is nothing more than a **behavioral choice**.

THE FOUNDERS ON HOMOSEXUALITY

The Founding Fathers of these United States would be incredulous, incensed, and outraged. They understood that acceptance of homosexuality would undermine and erode the moral foundations of civilization. Sodomy, the longtime historical term for same-sex relations, was a capital crime under British common law. Sir William Blackstone, British attorney, jurist, law professor, and political philosopher, authored his monumental *Commentaries on the Laws of England* from 1765-1769. These commentaries became the premiere legal source admired and used by America's Founding Fathers. In Book the Fourth, Chapter the Fifteenth, "Of Offences Against the Persons of Individuals," Blackstone stated:

William Blackstone

IV. WHAT has been here observed..., which ought to be the more clear in proportion **as the crime is the more detestable**, may be applied to another offence, of **a still deeper malignity**; **the infamous crime against nature**, committed either with man or beast.... But it is **an offence of so dark a nature**...that the accusation should be clearly made out....

I WILL not act so disagreeable part, to my readers as well as myself, as to dwell any longer upon a subject, **the very mention of which is a disgrace to human nature**. It will be more eligible to imitate in this respect the delicacy of our English law, which treats it, in its very indictments, as a crime not fit to be named; *peccatum illud horribile, inter chriftianos non nominandum* ["that horrible sin not to be named among Christians"— DM]. A taciturnity observed likewise by the edict of Constantius and Constans: *ubi fcelus eft id, quod non proficit fcire, jubemus infurgere leges, armari jura gladio ultore, ut exquifitis poenis fubdantur infames, qui* *funt, vel qui futuri funt, rei* ["When that crime is found, which is not profitable to know, we order the law to bring forth, to provide justice by force of arms with an avenging sword, that the infamous men be subjected to the due punishment, those who are found, or those who future will be found, in the deed"—DM]. Which leads me to add a work concerning its punishment.

THIS the voice of nature and of reason, and the express law of God, determine to be **capital**. Of which we have a signal instance, long before the Jewish dispensation, by the destruction of two cities by fire from heaven: so that this is an universal, not merely a provincial, precept. And our ancient law in some degree imitated this punishment, by **commanding such miscreants to be burnt to death**; though Fleta says they should be **buried alive**: either of which punishments was indifferently used for this crime among the ancient Goths. But now the general punishment of all felonies is the same, namely, **by hanging**: and this offence (being in the times of popery only subject to ecclesiastical censures) was made single felony by the statute 25 Hen. VIII. c. 6. and felony without benefit of clergy by statute 5 Eliz. c. 17. And the rule of law herein is, that, if both are arrived at years of discretion, *agentes et confentientes pari poena plectantur* ["advocates and conspirators should be punished with like punishment"—DM] (1769, 4.15.215-216, emp. added).

Here was the law of England—common law—under which Americans lived prior to achieving independence. That law did not change after gaining independence. To say the least, such thinking is hardly "politically correct" by today's standards.

How many Americans realize that while serving as the Commander-in-Chief of the Continental Army during the Revolutionary War, the Father of our country was apprised of a homosexual in the army? The response of General Washington was immediate and decisive. He issued "General Orders" from Army Headquarters at Valley Forge on Saturday, March 14, 1778:

> At a General Court Martial whereof Colo. Tupper was President (10th March 1778) Lieutt. Enslin of Colo. Malcom's Regiment tried for at-

Images courtesy of Library of Congress, Manuscript Division

tempting to commit <u>sodomy</u>, with John Monhort a soldier; Secondly, For Perjury in swearing to false Accounts, found guilty of the charges exhibited against him, being breaches of 5th Article 18th Section of the Articles of War **and do sentence him to be dismiss'd the service with Infamy**. His Excellency the Commander in Chief approves the sentence and **with Abhorrence and Detestation of such Infamous Crimes** orders Lieutt. Enslin **to be drummed out of Camp** tomorrow morning by all the Drummers and Fifers in the Army **never to return**; The Drummers and Fifers to attend on the Grand Parade at Guard mounting for that Purpose ("George...," underline in orig., emp. added).

Observe that the Father of our country viewed "sodomy" (the 18th-century word for homosexual relations) "with **Abhorrence and Detestation**."

Homosexuality was treated as a criminal offense in all of the original 13 colonies, and eventually every one of the 50 states (see Robinson, 2003; "Sodomy Laws...," 2003). Severe penalties were invoked for those who engaged in homosexuality. In fact, few Americans know that the penalty for homosexuality in several states was **death**—including New York, Vermont, Connecticut, and South Carolina (Barton, 2002, pp. 306,482). Most people nowadays would be shocked to learn that Thomas Jefferson advocated "dismemberment" as the penalty for homosexuality in his home state of Virginia, and even authored a bill to that effect (1781, Query 14; cf. 1903, 1:226-227).

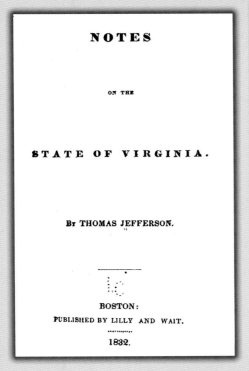

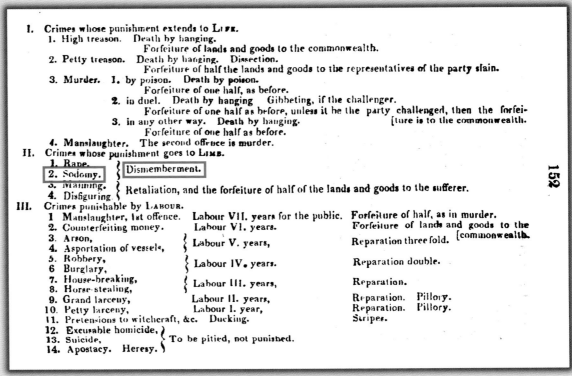

Images courtesy of Library of Congress, General Collections

Where did the Founding Fathers and early American citizenry derive their views on homosexuality? The historically unequivocal answer is—the Bible. "Traditional" (i.e., biblical) marriage in this country has always been between a man and a woman. In the words of Jesus: "Have you not read that He who made them at the beginning 'made them **male and female**,' and said, 'For this reason a man shall leave his father and mother and be joined to his wife, and the two shall become one flesh'?" (Matthew 19:4-5, emp. added). He was merely quoting the statement made by God regarding His creation of the first man and woman (Genesis 1:27; 2:24). God created Adam and Eve—not Adam and Steve, or Eve and Ellen. And throughout the rest of biblical history, God's attitude toward same-sex relations remained the same (Miller, et al., 2003).

In the greater scheme of human history, as civilizations have proceeded down the usual pathway of moral deterioration and eventual demise, the acceptance of same-sex relations has typically triggered the final stages of impending social implosion. America is being brought to the very brink of moral destruction. It would appear that the warning issued by God to the Israelites regarding their own ability to sustain their national existence in the Promised Land is equally apropos for America:

You shall not lie with a male as with a woman. It is an abomination.... Do not defile yourselves with any of these things; for by all these the nations are defiled, **which I am casting out before you**. For the land is defiled; therefore **I visit the punishment of its iniquity upon it, and the land vomits out its inhabitants**. You shall therefore keep My statutes and My judgments, and shall not commit any of these abominations...**lest the land vomit you out also** when you defile it, as it vomited out the nations that were before you (Leviticus 18:22-28, emp. added).

Mark this down, too: ***THE GOD OF THE BIBLE WILL NOT ALLOW THE ABOMINATION OF HOMOSEXUALITY TO GO UNCHALLENGED AND UNPUNISHED.*** Unless something is done to stop the moral degeneration, America would do well to prepare for the inevitable, divine expulsion.

SUMMARY

The butchery of babies and sexual perversion undoubtedly will go down in history as primary contributors to the moral and spiritual deterioration, decline, and collapse of American society (see Miller, 2006b). Abortion and homosexuality are glaring proofs of the expanding rejection of God in American civilization. They show the extent to which Americans are severing themselves from the laws of God in exchange for wanton indulgence of human passion. Forget where a candidate stands on health care, the environment, and social security! We simply must lay aside all the other political issues that vie for our attention and affect our finances, and vote based on where a candidate stands on these two premiere moral issues that will spell the doom of our nation. If the nation is punished for its moral degradation, our finances will be the least of our worries.

The Founders were adamant in their insistence that the survival of the Republic depends on its citizens maintaining Christian moral virtue. At a time when French immorality was notorious, John Jay related two experiences he had while in France:

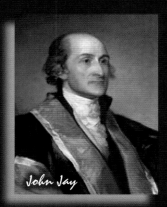

John Jay

> During my residence there, I do not recollect to have had more than two conversations with atheists about their tenets. The first was this: I was at a large party, of which were several of that description. **They spoke freely and contemptuously of religion.** I took no part in the conversation. In the course of it, one of them asked me if I believed in Christ? **I answered that I did, and that I thanked God that I did**…. Some
>
> time afterward, one of my family being dangerously ill, I was advised to send for an English physician who had resided many years at Paris…. But, it was added, he is an atheist…. [D]uring one of his visits, [he] very abruptly remarked that there was no God and he hoped the time would come when there would be no religion in the world. I very concisely remarked that **if there was no God there could be no moral obligations, and I did not see how society could subsist without them**… (as quoted in Jay, 1833, 2:346-347, emp. added).

Patrick Henry shared Jay's assessment of France. In fact, Henry, who "realized as few men did the danger to the republican institutions of his country from the undermining influence of French infidelity, set himself to counteracting its baneful influence by every means in his power" (1891, 2:200). Hear his forthright denunciation of French morals:

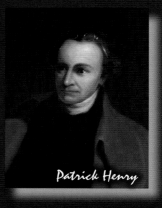

Patrick Henry

> But, as to France, I have no doubt in saying, that to her it will be calamitous. Her conduct has made it the interest of the great family of mankind to wish the downfall of her present government; because its existence is incompatible with that of all others within its reach. And, whilst I see the dangers that threaten ours from her intrigues and her arms, I am not so much alarmed as at **the apprehension of her destroying the great pillars of all government and of social life; I mean virtue, morality, and religion. This is the armor, my friend, and this alone, that renders us invincible. These are the tactics we should study. If we lose these, we are conquered, fallen indeed** (1891, 2:591-592, emp. added).

After serving two terms as Vice-President alongside President George Washington, the second President of these United States, John Adams, delivered a speech to military officers of the First Brigade of the Third Division of the Militia of Massachusetts on October 11, 1798, which included an uncompromising affirmation of the essentiality of Christian morality:

John Adams

> We have no government armed with power capable of contending with **human passions unbridled by morality and religion**…. Our constitution was made only for **a moral and religious people**. It is wholly inadequate to the government of any other (1854, 9:229, emp. added).

In a letter written from Philadelphia to the Abbés Chalut and Arnoux on April 17, 1787, Benjamin Franklin spoke positively of the relative calmness with which Americans were handling the "overturning" caused by the Revolution, which he attributed to America's stable moral framework::

> Your reflections on our situation compared with that of many nations of Europe, are very sensible and just. Let me add, that **only a virtuous people are capable of freedom. As nations become corrupt and vicious, they have more need of masters** (1988, emp. added).

Declaration signer and president of the Continental Congress (1784), Richard Henry Lee, emphatically affirmed on March 6, 1786: "It is certainly true that a popular government **cannot flourish without virtue in the people**" (1914, 2:411, emp. added). Dr. Benjamin Rush added his blunt observation: "Without the restraints of religion and social worship, **men become savages**" (1951, 1:505, emp. added).

In his critique of France's revolution, Founder Noah Webster spoke with displeasure of the French revolutionists' "impious attempts to exterminate every part of the Christian religion," and, referring to himself in the third person, insisted:

> He is not yet convinced that men are capable of such perfection on earth, as to regulate all their actions by moral rectitude, **without the restraints of religion and law**. He does not believe with the French atheist, that the universe is composed solely of matter and motion, without a Supreme Intelligence; nor that man is solely the creature of education. He believes that **God, and not education, gives man his passions**; and that the business of education is **to restrain and direct the passions to the purposes of social happiness**. He believes that man will always have passions—that these passions will frequently urge him into vices—**that religion has an excellent effect in repressing vices, in softening the manners of men**, and consoling them under the pressure of calamities (1794, Vol. 2, Ch. 44, emp. added).

All of these Founders, and many more, understood and believed the biblical declaration: "Righteousness exalts a nation, but sin is a reproach to any people" (Proverbs 14:34). We must rise up and petition political authorities in behalf of Christian morality. We have an evangelistic responsibility!

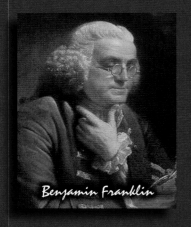

Benjamin Franklin

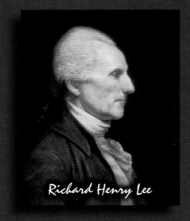

Richard Henry Lee

Benjamin Rush

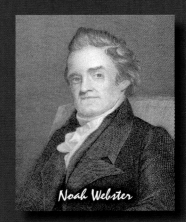

Noah Webster

Consider the solemn, virtually prophetic, warning issued by James A. Garfield, who became the 20th President of the United States in 1880:

> Now, more than ever before, **the people are responsible for the character of their Congress**. If that body be ignorant, reckless, and corrupt, it is because the people tolerate ignorance, recklessness, and corruption. If it be intelligent, brave, and pure, it is because the people demand these high qualities to represent them in the national legislature.... If the next centennial does not find us a great nation...it will be because **those who represent the enterprise, the culture, and the morality of the nation do not aid in controlling the political forces** (as quoted in Taylor, 1970, p. 180, emp. added).

James A. Garfield

And consider the relevant advice of the first Chief Justice of the first U.S. Supreme Court, John Jay, who, in a letter to Jedidiah Morse on January 1, 1813, commented on whether Christians should elect non-Christians to public office:

> Whether our religion permits Christians to vote for infidel rulers is a question which merits more consideration than it seems yet to have generally received either from the clergy or the laity. It appears to me that what the prophet said to Jehoshaphat about his attachment to Ahab affords a salutary lesson (1890, 4:365).

Jay was referring to the query posed by Jehu: "Should you help the wicked and love those who hate the Lord?" (2 Chronicles 19:2). Jay further insisted that Americans must be diligent in their political selections since it was God who gave us this privilege:

> Providence has given to our people the choice of their rulers. It is the duty, as well as the privilege and interest, of

our Christian nation to select and prefer **Christians for their rulers** (as quoted in Jay, 1833, 2:376, emp. added).

Founder Noah Webster was in complete agreement:

> [L]et it be impressed on your mind that **God commands you to choose for rulers just men who will rule in the fear of God** [an allusion to Exodus 18:21—DM]. The preservation of a republican government depends on the faithful discharge of this duty; if the citizens neglect their duty and place unprincipled men in office, the government will soon be corrupted.... If a republican government fails to secure public prosperity and happiness, **it must be because the citizens neglect the Divine commands and elect bad men to make and administer the laws** (1832, pp. 336-337, emp. added).

Jethro told his son-in-law, Moses, four critical qualifications for political leaders that square with God's view of the matter: "Moreover you shall select from all the people **able men**, such as **fear God**, men of **truth**, hating **covetousness**" (Exodus 18:21, emp. added). Or as Solomon stated: "When the righteous are in authority, the people rejoice; But when a wicked man rules, the people groan.... The king establishes the land by justice, but he who receives bribes overthrows it" (Proverbs 29:2,4).

The fact is, **we had better forget politics and party loyalties**, and learn to think and act **spiritually**. We must view political issues from the perspective of God as indicated in His Word (Isaiah 55:8-9; Jeremiah 10:23). We must learn to make decisions in harmony with Christian morals and principles. Signer of the *Declaration* and physician, Dr. Benjamin Rush, put this matter in perspective:

> I have been alternately called an aristocrat and a democrat. I am neither. **I am a Christocrat**. I believe all pow-

er...will always fail of producing order and happiness in the hands of man. He alone who created and redeemed man is qualified to govern him (as quoted in Ramsay, 1813, p. 103, emp. added).

VI. Boycott Hollywood. Do not enable the entertainment industry in its wicked assault on morality. Hollywood does not represent what America has always been about. In fact, they are as antagonistic and hostile toward God, Christianity, and true patriotism as anyone can be. And many Americans are insanely enamored with the fluff and glitter of such frivolous pursuits. Indeed, with the passing of the World War II generation, succeeding generations of Americans have come on the scene who have little interest in the higher, nobler aspects of human existence, cultivating moral excellence and the virtuous development of the human spirit. Instead, entertainment, pleasure, physical stimulation, and indulging fleshly appetites now take center stage. To show the extent to which Americans have degenerated in their sensibilities, who would have ever imagined that the day could ever come when an *American Idol* contestant would generate more votes than any U.S. President has received (August, et al., 2006, p. 23)? **We ought to be ashamed—and alarmed**. Does recreation and playing mean more to us than our souls, the souls of our children, and the survival of our society?

VII. Be resolute, steadfast, and unmovable. Do not give up. Stay with the battle. America's current condition did not develop overnight. It will take time and persistence to turn the nation around.

To capsule these seven items: **STAND UP AND SPEAK OUT**! Verbalize and articulate the truth at every opportunity. The solution to all of the problems encountered by humans is the Word of God. The Bible has the answers!

CONCLUSION

What lies ahead for America when a sizable percentage of the citizenry no longer acknowledges or submits to the God of the Bible? What is going to happen to this country when many of our people no longer believe that a nation is blessed only if its God is the Lord? What does the future hold, given the direction we are going? **The Founders anticipated and answered these very questions**. Prepare yourself. On March 11, 1792, the Father of our country made the following statement—one that is particularly chilling in view of the specter of terrorism that hangs over the nation:

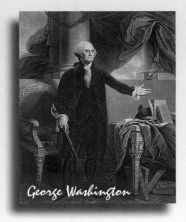

George Washington

I am sure there never was a people who had more reason **to acknowledge a Divine interposition in their affairs** than those of the United States; and I should be pained to believe that **they have forgotten that Agency** which was so often manifested during our revolution, or that they failed to consider the omnipotence of that God **who is alone able to protect them** (Washington, 1838, 10:222-223, emp. added).

Undoubtedly, America has the greatest, most technologically sophisticated military in human history. Yet, according to the first Commander-in-Chief of America's armed forces, God **alone** is able to protect the country. He was merely echoing Scripture. Read carefully the words of the psalmist:

No king is saved by the multitude of an army; a mighty man is not delivered by great strength. A horse is a vain hope for safety; neither shall it deliver any by its great strength. Behold, the eye of the Lord is on **those who fear Him**, on **those who hope in His mercy**, to deliver their soul from death, and to keep them alive in famine (Psalm 33:16-19, emp. added).

In the final analysis, all of the Apache attack helicopters, Tomahawk subsonic cruise missiles, nuclear warheads, and sophisticated military weaponry that American ingenuity has created, will not save America. Rather, only God can preserve us—and His protective care is extended only to **those who fear Him**. But should we make preparations for defense? Certainly. The Bible declares: "The horse is **prepared** for the day of battle, but deliverance is of the Lord" (Proverbs 21:31, emp. added). Sure, we should make preparations for the defense of the nation against outside forces; but we must keep ever before us the fact that deliverance from enemies comes ultimately from God—not man. And God extends His assistance to the virtuous and righteous—as noted by Patrick Henry:

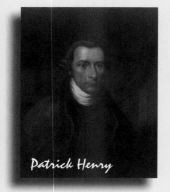

Patrick Henry

> Whether this will prove a blessing or a curse, will depend upon the use our people make of the blessings which a gracious God hath bestowed on us. If they are wise, they will be great and happy. If they are of a contrary character, they will be miserable. Righteousness **alone** can exalt them as a nation. Reader! Whoever thou art, remember this; and in thy sphere practice virtue thyself, and encourage it in others" (as quoted in Henry, 1891, 1:81-82, emp. added). "The great pillars of all government and of social life: I mean virtue, morality, and religion. **This is the armor, my friend, and this alone, that renders us invincible**" (1891, 2:592, emp. added).

John Witherspoon echoed precisely the same sentiment: "He who makes a people virtuous makes them invincible" (1815, 9:231).

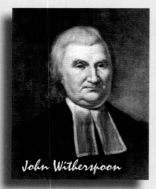

John Witherspoon

Another uncanny, prophetic warning was issued by Jedidiah Morse, the "Father of American Geography" and father of Samuel Morse, the inventor of the Morse Code (see "Morse, Jedidiah," 2007). In an election sermon given at Charlestown, Massachusetts on April 25, 1799, this American patriot offered the following frightening warning—an observation not unlike those of many of the Founders:

Jedidiah Morse

The foundations which support the interest of Christianity, are also necessary to support a free and equal government like our own. In all those countries where there is little or no religion, or a very gross and corrupt one, as in Mahometan and Pagan countries, there you will find, with scarcely a single exception, arbitrary and tyrannical governments, gross ignorance and wickedness, and deplorable wretchedness among the people. **To the kindly influence of Christianity we owe that degree of civil freedom, and political and social happiness which mankind now enjoy**. In proportion as the genuine effects of Christianity are diminished in any nation, either through unbelief, or the corruption of its doctrines, or the neglect of its institutions; **in the same proportion will the people of that nation recede from the blessings of genuine freedom, and approximate the miseries of complete despotism**. I hold this to be a truth confirmed by experience. If so, it follows, that all efforts made to destroy the foundations of our holy religion, ultimately tend to the subversion also of our political freedom and happiness. **Whenever the pillars of Christianity shall be overthrown, our present republican forms of government, and all the blessings which flow from them, must fall with them** (1799, p. 9, emp. added).

Recall the somber warning of *Declaration* signer Charles Carroll of Carrollton, in a letter written to fellow Founder and signer of the federal *Constitution*, James McHenry, on November 4, 1800:

Charles Carroll

Without morals a republic cannot subsist any length of time; they therefore who are decrying the Christian religion, whose morality is so sublime and pure...are undermining the solid foundation of morals, **the best security for the duration of free governments** (as quoted in Steiner, 1907, p. 475, emp. added).

Noah Webster sounded the same warning:

> [T]he Christian religion, in it purity, is the basis, or rather the source of all genuine freedom in government.... and I am persuaded that no civil government of a republican form **can exist and be durable** in which the principles of that religion have not a controlling influence (as quoted in Snyder, 1990, p. 253, emp. added).

Elias Boudinot, president of the Continental Congress (1782-1783), articulated the same precise point, when he expressed his "anxious desire" that:

> our country should be preserved from the dreadful evil of becoming enemies to the religion of the Gospel, which I have no doubt, but would be introductive of **the dissolution of government and the bonds of civil society** (1801, p. xxii, emp. added).

Declaration signer and Connecticut governor, Samuel Huntington, agreed, as indicated by his remarks on January 9, 1788 at the state convention debating ratification of the federal *Constitution*:

> While the great body of freeholders are acquainted with the duties which they owe to their God, to themselves,

and to men, they will remain free. **But if ignorance and depravity should prevail, they will inevitably lead to slavery and ruin** (as quoted in Elliott, 1836, 2:200, emp. added).

Signer of the *Constitution*, Gouverneur Morris, insisted in a speech delivered September 4, 1816:

> There must be religion. When that ligament is torn, **society is disjointed and its members perish**. The nation is exposed to **foreign violence and domestic convulsion**. Vicious rulers, chosen by vicious people, turn back the current of corruption to its source. Placed in a situation where they can exercise authority for their own emolument, they betray their trust. They take bribes. They sell statutes and decrees. They sell honor and office. They sell their conscience. They sell their country. By this vile traffic they become odious and contemptible.... But the most important of all lessons is the denunciation of **ruin to every State that rejects the precepts of religion**" (1821, pp. 32,34, emp. added).

Declaration signer and "The Father of the American Revolution," Samuel Adams, likewise issued a solemn warning in a letter to James Warren on February 12, 1779:

> A general dissolution of the principles and manners will more surely overthrow the liberties of America than the whole force of the common enemy. While the people are virtuous, they cannot be subdued; but when once they lose their virtue, **they will be ready to surrender their**

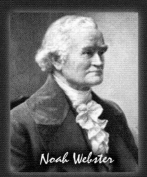
Noah Webster

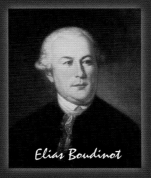
Elias Boudinot

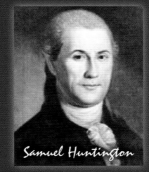
Samuel Huntington

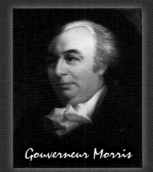
Gouverneur Morris

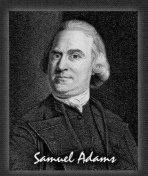
Samuel Adams

liberties to the first external or internal invader** (1908, 4:124, emp. added).

In his inaugural address as the Governor of Massachusetts in 1780, Founder John Hancock insisted that both our freedom and our very existence as a Republic will be determined by public attachment to Christian morality:

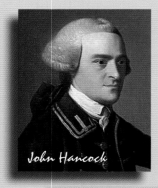

John Hancock

> Sensible of **the importance of Christian piety and virtue** to the order and happiness of a state, I cannot but earnestly commend to you every measure for their support and encouragement.... Manners, by which not only the freedom, but **the very existence of the republics**, are greatly affected, depend much upon the public institutions of religion and the good education of youth (as quoted in Brown, 1898, p. 269, emp. added).

Revolutionary War soldier and U.S. Federal judge appointed by President John Adams, Jeremiah Smith, declared in an oration on February 22, 1800:

> [C]herish and promote the interest of knowledge, virtue and religion. They are **indispensable to the support of any free government**.... Let it never be forgotten that **there can be no genuine freedom** where there is no morality, and no sound morality **where there is no religion**" (as quoted in Atherton, 1800, p. 81, emp. added).

The words of *Declaration* signer John Witherspoon are frightening: "Nothing is more certain than that a general profligacy

and corruption of manners make a people **ripe for destruction**" (1802, 3:41, emp. added).

Observe: according to the Framers and Founders, the American republic cannot last any length of time without Christian morals characterizing the people; no civil government of a republic can exist and last without the controlling influence of Christian principles; the government and civility in society would dissolve if the citizens become enemies of Christianity; ignorance of one's duty to God and depravity will lead to slavery and ruin; without religion, foreign violence, domestic convulsion, and ruin result; abandoning Christian virtue will result in submission to invaders; there can be no genuine freedom where religion and morality are lost; and we will then be ripe for destruction. There is no doubt that the Founders were single-minded in their recognition of the same fact: if Christianity, Christian morality, and devotion to the God of the Bible dissipate in America, **we cannot perpetuate our national existence—and the nation is doomed**.

In a speech delivered on February 23, 1852, second generation American, Daniel Webster, likewise warned what would happen to America if she ever displaced God from His rightful position over the nation. His words are eerily prophetic in that they now describe America to a T:

> [I]f we and our posterity reject religious instruction and authority, violate the rules of eternal justice, trifle with the injunctions of morality, and recklessly destroy the political constitution which holds us together, **no man can tell how sudden a catastrophe may overwhelm us that shall bury all our glory in profound obscurity** (1903, 13:492-493, emp. added).

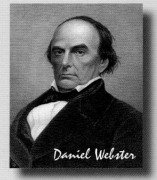

Daniel Webster

Luther Martin

George Mason

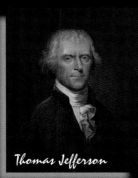

Thomas Jefferson

Ask yourself four questions—**#1**: Are Americans—on a widespread scale—**rejecting Christian instruction and authority**? *The polls show that fewer and fewer attend church service or follow the Bible.* **#2**: Are Americans **violating the rules of eternal justice**? *Look at the unprecedented numbers of lawbreakers occupying overcrowded prisons, and the shift in the justice system that commenced in the 1960s favoring the "rights" of the criminal.* **#3**: Are Americans **trifling with the injunctions of morality**? *Unbelievably, we are actually having a national discussion (battle) on how to define marriage!* **#4**: Are Americans **recklessly destroying the Constitution**? *Liberal Supreme Court justices reject strict constructionist interpretation and insist on looking to the courts of the world for their opinions, while federal judges are legislating from the bench—even overriding majority votes of the people.* The haunting answer to these four questions is a resounding "Yes!" *How, then, can we as a nation possibly escape catastrophe*? We cannot. We will not.

In view of how God has dealt with nations in world history, and in view of the fact that "God still rules in the kingdoms of men" (Daniel 4:17), we ought to expect God to react to America's degradation in two ways: (1) unleash upon (or at least cease to protect) the country (or specific localities within the country) natural disasters (read the Old Testament book of Joel); or (2) allow hostile enemies to inflict casualties and suffering upon us (read Habakkuk). It is interesting that the Founding Fathers recognized this eternal principle as having been posited in the fabric of the Universe by the Creator. They understood that while God will judge each individual human being at the Judgment when Christ returns (e.g., 2 Corinthians 5:10), He judges nations **in history, in time**, by bringing destruction upon them when their iniquity is "full" (Genesis 15:16; cf. Miller, 2005). That is why Luther Martin, a delegate to the federal Constitutional Convention, stated in 1788: "It was said, it ought to be considered, that national crimes can only be, and frequently are, **punished in this world by national punishments**" (as quoted in Elliott, 1836, 1:374, emp. added). As the Father of the Bill of Rights, George Mason, affirmed to his fellow delegates to the Constitutional Convention on August 22, 1787: "As nations cannot be rewarded or punished in the next world, so they must be in this. By an inevitable chain of causes and effects, **Providence punishes national sins by national calamities**" (as quoted in Madison, 1840, 3:1391, emp. added). The "Father of the American Revolution" and signer of the *Declaration of Independence*, Samuel Adams, explained: "Revelation assures us that 'Righteousness exalteth a nation.' Communities are dealt with **in this world** by the wise and just Ruler of the Universe. **He rewards or punishes them** according to their general character" (1907, 3:286, emp. added). Thomas Jefferson likewise warned: "I tremble for my country when I reflect that God is just: that **His justice cannot sleep forever**" (1781, Query 18, p. 237, emp. added).

Observe carefully how the words of Judges 2:10 so aptly describe the cataclysmic shift that has taken place in America between the World War II generation—considered by some "the greatest generation any society has ever produced" ("Tom Brokaw...")—and those that have come after: "When all that generation had been gathered to their fathers, another generation arose after them who did not know the Lord nor the work which He had done for Israel." Since World War II, succeeding generations of Americans no longer acknowledge God and Christ, and they are woefully ignorant of what God has done for America. The Founders would have had a hard time imagining that such could ever happen here, as George Washington expressed on June 29, 1788:

> No country upon earth ever had it more in its power to attain these blessings than United America. Wondrously strange, then, and much to be regretted indeed would it be, were we to neglect the means and to depart from the road which Providence has pointed us to so plainly; **I cannot believe it will ever come to pass** (Series 2, Letterbook 15, Image 172, emp. added).

A similar, striking resemblance may be seen in the warning God issued to Solomon and the nation over which he served as king:

> [I]f My people who are called by My name will humble themselves, and pray and seek My face, and turn from their wicked ways, then I will hear from heaven, and will forgive their sin and heal their land. Now My eyes will be open and My ears attentive to prayer made in this place…. But **if you turn away and forsake My statutes and My commandments which I have set before you, and go and serve other gods, and worship them**, then I will uproot them from My land which I have given them; and this house which I have sanctified for My name I will cast out of My sight, and will make it a proverb and a byword among all peoples…. [E]veryone who passes by it will be astonished and say, "Why has the Lord done thus to this land and this house?" Then they will answer, "Because they forsook the Lord God of their fathers…and embraced other gods, and worshiped them and served them; **therefore He has brought all this calamity on them** (2 Chronicles 7:14-22, emp. added; cf. Deuteronomy 29:19-28).

As the population of America continues its progressive entrenchment against God, the outcome is inevitable: "The wicked shall be turned into hell, and **all nations that forget God**" (Psalm 9:17, emp. added). Indeed, as Americans turn their back on the God of their fathers, so God will cease to bestow His protection and blessings. "'Shall I not punish them for these things?' says the Lord. 'Shall I not avenge Myself on such a nation as this?'" (Jeremiah 5:9,29; 9:9). The only hope for America is to experience a nationwide spiritual awakening by returning to God and begging His forgiveness. "'Return to Me, and I will return to you,' says the Lord of hosts" (Malachi 3:7). Our only hope is for a sizeable percentage of Americans to rise up and act upon the factuality of the psalmist's words: "Let all the earth fear the Lord; Let all the inhabitants of the world stand in awe of Him…. **Blessed is the nation whose God is the Lord**" (Psalm 33:8,12). God help us. If it be His will, may God save the United States of America.

REFERENCES

"Abortion and Birth Control" (2008), Polling Report, [On-line], URL: http://www.pollingreport.com/abortion.htm.

"About Yale" (no date), Yale University, [On-line], URL: http://www.yale.edu/about/history.html.

Adams, John (1797), "Inaugural Address," The Avalon Project at Yale Law School, [On-line], URL: http://www.yale.edu/lawweb/avalon/presiden/inaug/adams.htm.

Adams, John (1850-1856), *The Works of John Adams, Second President of the United States*, ed. Charles Adams (Boston, MA: Little, Brown, & Company).

Adams, John Quincy (1821), *Address Delivered at the Request of the Committee of Arrangements for Celebrating the Anniversary of Independence at the City of Washington on the Fourth of July 1821, Upon the Occasion of the Reading the Declaration of Independence* (Cambridge: Hilliard and Metcalf), [On-line], URL: http://digital.library.umsystem.edu/cgi/t/text/text-idx?sid=b80c023f0007f89b5b95e4be026fa267;c=jul;idno=jul000087.

Adams, John Quincy (1837), *An Oration Delivered Before the Inhabitants of the Town of Newburyport, at Their Request, on the Sixty-first Anniversary of the Declaration of Independence, July 4th, 1837* (Newburyport, MA: Charles Whipple).

Adams, Samuel (1904-1908), *The Writings of Samuel Adams*, ed. Harry Cushing (New York: G.P. Putnam's Sons).

Adams, Samuel and John Adams (1802), *Four Letters: Being an Interesting Correspondence Between Those Eminently Distinguished Characters, John Adams, Late President of the United States; and Samuel Adams, Late Governor of Massachusetts. On the Important Subject of Government* (Boston, MA: Adams and Rhoades).

Adler, Mortimer, ed. (1968), *The Annals of America* (Chicago, IL: Encyclopedia Britannica).

"America the Beautiful," [On-line], URL: http://www.niehs.nih.gov/kids/lyrics/america.htm#history.

Annals of Congress (1789), "Amendments to the Constitution," June 8, [On-line], URL: http://memory.loc.gov/cgi-bin/ampage?collId=llac& fileName=001/llac001.db&rec Num=221.

"Appendix C: Members of the Joint Commission," Washington Monument: A History, [On-line], URL: http://www.nps.gov/wamo/history/appc.htm.

Atherton, Charles (1800), *A Selection of Orations and Eulogies Pronounced in Different Parts of the United States In Commemoration of the Life, Virtue, and Preeminent Services of Gen. George Washington* (Amherst, NY: Samuel Preston).

August, Melissa, et al. (2006), "Milestones," *Time*, 167[23]:June 5.

Barton, David (2002), *Original Intent* (Aledo, TX: Wallbuilders), 3rd edition.

"Battle Hymn of the Republic," [On-line], URL: http://www.cyberhymnal.org/htm/b/h/bhymnotr.htm.

Beardsley, Edwards (1886), *Life and Times of William Samuel Johnson* (Boston, MA: Houghton, Mifflin & Co.).

Bedford, Gunning (1800), *Funeral Oration Upon the Death of General George Washington* (Wilmington, NC: James Wilson).

"The Bible" (no date), [On-line], URL: http://www.xphomestation.com/frm-history.html.

Blackstone, William (1769), *Commentaries on the Laws of England*, [On-line], URL: http://www.yale.edu/lawweb/avalon/blackstone/bk4ch15.htm.

"Blue law" (2008), *Encyclopædia Britannica Online,* [On-line], URL: http://www.britannica.com/EBchecked/topic/70275/blue-law.

Boudinot, Elias (1801), *The Age of Revelation* (Philadelphia, PA: Asbury Dickins), [On-line], URL: http://www.google.com/books?id=Xpc PAAAAIAAJ.

Boudinot, Elias (1896), *The Life, Public Services, Addresses, and Letters of Elias Boudinot, President of the Continental Congress*, ed. J.J. Boudinot (Boston, MA: Houghton, Mifflin).

Boutell, Lewis (1896), *The Life of Roger Sherman* (Chicago, IL: A.C. McClurg).

Bowers v. Hardwick, 478 U.S. 186 (1986), [On-line], URL: http://caselaw.lp.findlaw.com/scripts/getcase.pl?court=us&vol=478&invol=186.

Brown, Abram (1898), *John Hancock, His Book* (Boston, MA: Lee & Shepard Publishers), [On-line], URL: http://www.archive.org/details/johnhancock00browrich.

"Cemeteries," American Battle Monuments Commission, [On-line], URL: http://www.abmc.gov/cemeteries/index.php.

Charter of Connecticut (1662), The Avalon Project at Yale Law School, [On-line], URL: http://www.yale.edu/lawweb/avalon/states/ct03.htm.

Charter of Dartmouth College (1769), Dartmouth College Government Documents, [On-line], URL: http://www.dartmouth.edu/~govdocs/case/charter.htm.

"Chief Justice Roy Moore" (2003), [On-line], URL: http://www.retakingamerica.com/great_amer_ten_moore_001.html.

Church of the Holy Trinity v. United States, 143 U.S. 457; 12 S. Ct. 511; 36 L. Ed. 226; 1892 U.S. LEXIS 2036.

Clancy, Michael (2001), "Story of the 'Fetal Hand Grasp' Photograph," [On-line], URL: http://www.michaelclancy.com/story.html.

Cohn, Henry S. (1988), "Connecticut Constitutional History: 1636-1776," Connecticut State Library, [On-line], URL: http://www.cslib.org/cts4cc.htm#1.

Collections of the New York Historical Society for the Year 1821 (1821), (New York: E. Bliss & E. White).

"Common Era" (2008), *Encyclopædia Britannica Online,* [On-line], URL: http://www.britannica.com/EBchecked/topic/128268/Common-Era.

"Congress Confirms 'God' in Pledge, Motto" (2002), [On-line], URL: http://usgovinfo.about.com/library/weekly/aa101602a.htm.

Constitution of the American Bible Society (1816), (New York: ABS).

Constitution of the Commonwealth of Massachusetts, [On-line], URL: http://www.mass.gov/legis/const.htm.

Constitution of Connecticut (1818), State of Connecticut, [On-line], URL: http://www.sots.state.ct.us/RegisterManual/SectionI/1818CTCO.HTM.

Constitution of the State of Maine, [On-line], URL: http://www.state.me.us/sos/arc/general/constit/conspre.htm.

"Continental Currency: 1778 $60 Note," Serial Number: 95,405, [On-line], URL: http://www.coins.nd.edu/ColCurrency/CurrencyImages/CC/CC-09-26-78-$60.obv.jpg.

"Continental Currency: 1779 $30 Note," Serial Number: 51,381, [On-line], URL: http://www.coins.nd.edu/ColCurrency/CurrencyImages/CC/CC-01-14-79-$30.obv.jpg.

"Continental Currency: 1779 $40 Note," Serial Number: 171,449, [On-line], URL: http://www.coins.nd.edu/ColCurrency/CurrencyImages/CC/CC-01-14-79-$40.obv.jpg.

Coolidge, Calvin (1925), "Inaugural Address," The Avalon Project at Yale Law School, [On-line], URL: http://www.yale.edu/lawweb/avalon/presiden/inaug/coolidge.htm.

Davies, Samuel and Gilbert Tennent (1754 edition), *The Value of the College at Princeton: From A General Account of the Rise and State of the College, Lately Established in the Province of New Jersey*, [On-line], URL: http://personal.pitnet.net/primarysources/princeton.html.

The Declaration of Independence (1776), National Archives, [On-line], URL: http://www.archives.gov/national_archives_experience/charters/declaration.html.

Devorah, Carrie (2003), "God in the Temples of Government: Part I," [On-line], URL: http://www.humaneventsonline.com/article.php?id=2441.

Devorah, Carrie (2004), "God in the Temples of Government: Part II," [On-line], URL: http://www.papillonsartpalace.com/godinthe.htm.

"Dwight David Eisenhower" (no date), [On-line], URL: http://www.geocities.com/peterroberts.geo/Relig-Politics/DDEisenhower.html#ln.

Eighth Report of the Bible Society of Philadelphia (1816) (Philadelphia, PA: William Fry).

Elliott, Jonathan, ed. (1836), *The Debates in the Several State Conventions* (Washington, DC: Jonathan Elliott).

"FAQs: Currency Portraits and Designs," U.S. Department of the Treasury, [On-line], URL: http://www.ustreas.gov/education/faq/currency/portraits.shtml#q3.

"Federal Judge Rules Reciting Pledge in Schools Unconstitutional" (2005), *Fox News*, September 15, [On-line], URL: http://www.foxnews.com/story/0,2933,169379,00.html.

"Fort McHenry: Birthplace of our National Anthem," [On-line], URL: http://www.bcpl.net/~etowner/anthem.html.

Franklin, Benjamin (1787), "Constitutional Convention Address on Prayer," [On-line], URL: http://www.americanrhetoric.com/speeches/benfranklin.htm.

Franklin, Benjamin (1988), *The Papers of Benjamin Franklin (Digital Edition)*, ed. Barbara Oberg (Los Altos, CA: The Packard Humanities Institute), [On-line], URL: http://www.franklinpapers.org/franklin/.

"Frieze of American History," The Architect of the Capitol, [On-line], URL: http://www.aoc.gov/cc/art/rotunda/frieze/index.cfm.

Fundamental Agreement, or Original Constitution of the Colony of New Haven (1639), The Avalon Project at Yale Law School, [On-line], URL: http://www.yale.edu/lawweb/avalon/states/ct01.htm.

Fundamental Orders (1639), The Avalon Project at Yale Law School, [On-line], URL: http://www.yale.edu/lawweb/avalon/order.htm.

Gallagher, Maggie (2006), "Banned in Boston," *The Weekly Standard*, 11[33], May 15, [On-line], URL: http://www.weeklystandard.com/Content/Public/Articles/000/000/012/191 kgwgh.asp.

"Gay and Lesbian Issues" (2002), American Psychiatric Association Public Information, [On-line], URL: http://www.psych.org/public_info/homose-1.cfm.

"George Washington, March 14, 1778, General Orders" (1778), The George Washington Papers at the Library of Congress, 1741-1799, from ed. John C. Fitzpatrick, *The Writings of George Washington from the Original Manuscript Sources, 1745-1799,* [On-line], URL: http://memory.loc.gov/cgi-bin/query/r?ammem/mgw:@field(DOCID+@lit(gw110081)).

"The Great Seal and the National Mottos of the United States of America," U.S. Scouting Service Project, [On-line], URL: http://www.usscouts.org/flag/sealmotto.html.

Hamilton, Alexander (1961-1987), *The Papers of Alexander Hamilton*, ed. Harold Syrett (New York: Columbia University Press).

Harding, Warren G. (1921), "Inaugural Address," The Avalon Project at Yale Law School, [On-line], URL: http://www.yale.edu/lawweb/avalon/presiden/inaug/harding.htm.

Harrison, William Henry (1841), "Inaugural Address," The Avalon Project at Yale Law School, [On-line], URL: http://www.yale.edu/lawweb/avalon/presiden/inaug/harrison.htm.

Harrub, Brad and Dave Miller (2004), "'This is the Way God Made Me'—A Scientific Examination of Homosexuality and the 'Gay Gene,'" *Reason & Revelation*, 24[8]:73-79, August, [On-line], URL: http://www.apologeticspress.org/articles/2553.

Haynes, Charles C. (2006), "A Moral Battleground, A Civil Discourse," First Amendment Center, May 20, [On-line], URL: http://www.firstamendmentcenter.org/commentary.aspx?id=16664.

Henry, Patrick (1775), "Give Me Liberty Or Give Me Death," The Avalon Project at Yale Law School, [On-line], URL: http://www.yale.edu/lawweb/avalon/patrick.htm.

Henry, Patrick (1891), *Patrick Henry; Life, Correspondence and Speeches*, ed. William Henry (New York: Charles Scribner's Sons), [On-line], URL: http://www.archive.org/details/pathenrylife01henrrich.

Herek, Gregory (2002), "Facts about Homosexuality and Mental Health," [On-line], URL: http://psychology.ucdavis.edu/rainbow/html/facts_mental_health.html.

"History of 'In God We Trust,'" United States Department of the Treasury, [On-line], URL: http://www.ustreas.gov/education/fact-sheets/currency/in-god-we-trust.html.

"History of the Association" (no date), The Gideons International, [On-line], URL: http://www.gideons.org/.

Horton, Wesley (1988), "Connecticut Constitutional History: 1776-1988," Connecticut State Library, [On-line], URL: http://www.cslib.org/cts4ch.htm#1.

"House of Representatives Chamber" (no date), *Images of American Political History*, [On-line], URL: http://teachpol.tcnj.edu/amer_pol_hist/thumbnail513.html.

Hume, Brent (2005), "Prayer Punishment," Fox News Special Report, April 7, [On-line], URL: http://www.foxnews.com/story/0,2933,152684,00.html.

Imbody, Jonathan (2003), "A Flash of Life," *Free Republic*, October 31, [On-line], URL: http://freerepublic.com/focus/f-news/1012548/posts.

"Inaugurals of Presidents of the United States: Some Precedents and Notable Events," Library of Congress, [On-line], URL: http://rs6.loc.gov/ammem/pihtml/pinotable.html.

"In God We Trust," The Architect of the Capitol, Capitol Complex, [On-line], URL: http://www.aoc.gov/cc/plaques/in_god.cfm.

Jay, John (1890), *The Correspondence and Public Papers of John Jay, 1763-1781*, ed. Henry Johnston (New York: Burt Franklin).

Jay, John (1980), *John Jay: The Winning of the Peace. Unpublished Papers 1780-1784*, ed. Richard Morris (New York: Harper & Row).

Jay, William (1833), *The Life of John Jay* (New York: J. & J. Harper).

Jefferson, Thomas (1781), *Notes on the State of Virginia*, The Avalon Project at Yale Law School, [On-line], URL: http://www.yale.edu/lawweb/avalon/jevifram.htm.

Jefferson, Thomas (1801), "First Inaugural Address," The Avalon Project at Yale Law School, [On-line], URL: http://www.yale.edu/lawweb/avalon/presiden/inaug/jefinau1.htm.

Jefferson, Thomas (1802), "Thomas Jefferson to Danbury, Connecticut, Baptist Association," Library of Congress: The Thomas Jefferson Papers Series 1. General Correspondence, January 1, [On-line], URL: http://memory.loc.gov/cgi-bin/ampage?collId=mtj1&fileName=mtj1page025.db&recNum=557&itemLink=/ammem/mtjhtml/mtjser1.html&linkText=7&tempFile=./temp/~ammem_RsNQ&filecode=mtj&next_filecode=mtj&prev_filecode=mtj&itemnum=2&ndocs=22.

Jefferson, Thomas (1805), "Second Inaugural Address," The Avalon Project at Yale Law School, [On-line], URL: http://www.yale.edu/lawweb/avalon/presiden/inaug/jefinau2.htm.

Jefferson, Thomas (1903), *Writings of Thomas Jefferson*, ed. Albert Bergh (Washington, DC: Thomas Jefferson Memorial Association).

Johnson, Kirk (2005), "Colorado Court Bars Execution Because Jurors Consulted Bible," *New York Times*, A[5]:1, March 25.

Journals of the Continental Congress, 1774-1789 (1909), ed. Worthington C. Ford, et al. (Washington, D.C.: Government Printing Office), [On-line], URL: http://memory.loc.gov/cgi-bin/ampage.

Kent, James (1826), *Commentaries on American Law*, ed. Jon Roland (New York: O. Halsted), 15th edition, [On-line], URL: http://www.constitution.org/jk/jk_000.htm.

King, Rufus (1900), *The Life and Correspondence of Rufus King*, ed. Charles King (New York: G.P. Putnam's Sons).

"Laus Deo," [On-line], URL: http://www.ucmpage.org/articles/laus_deo.html.

"Lawmakers Blast Pledge Ruling" (2002), *CNN*, June 27, [On-line], URL: http://archives.cnn.com/2002/LAW/06/26/pledge.allegiance/.

Lawrence, et al. v. Texas, No. 02-102 (2003), [On-line], URL: http://caselaw.lp.findlaw.com/cgi-bin/getcase.pl?court=US&navby=case&vol=000&invol=02-102.

Lee, Richard Henry (1914), *The Letters of Richard Henry Lee*, ed. James Ballagh (New York: MacMillan).

"Legend for the Seal of the United States, August 1776" (1998), in "Religion and the Founding of the American Republic: Object List," Library of Congress, [On-line], URL: http://www.loc.gov/exhibits/religion/obj-list.html.

"The Liberty Bell," National Park Service, [On-line], URL: http://www.nps.gov/inde/liberty-bell.html.

"Lincoln: The Memorial," [On-line], URL: http://www.nps.gov/linc/memorial/memorial.htm#.

Lincoln, Abraham (1861), "First Inaugural Address," The Avalon Project at Yale Law School, [On-line], URL: http://www.yale.edu/lawweb/avalon/presiden/inaug/lincoln1.htm.

"List of University Mottos" (no date), Answers.com, [On-line], URL: http://www.answers.com/topic/list-of-university-mottos.

Lutz, Donald (1988), *The Origins of American Constitutionalism* (Baton Rouge, LA: Louisiana State University Press).

Lyons, Eric (2007), "Tiny Babies Abortionists Would Rather We Forget," Apologetics Press, [On-line], URL: http://www.apologeticspress.org/articles/3280.

Madison, James (1840), *The Papers of James Madison*, ed. Henry Gilpin (Washington, D.C.: Langtree & O'Sullivan).

"McGuffey Readers—Hard Cover Samples" (no date), [On-line], URL: http://www.howtotutor.com/samples1.htm.

"McGuffey's Reader" (2005), Ohio Historical Society, [On-line], URL: http://www.ohiohistorycentral.org/entry.php?rec=1469.

Miller, Dave (2003), "Abortion and the Bible," [On-line], URL: http://www.apologeticspress.org/articles/1964.

Miller, Dave (2004), "Babies, Eagles, and the Right to Live," Apologetics Press, [On-line]: URL: http://www.apologeticspress.org/rr/reprints/babyeagles.pdf.

Miller, Dave (2005), "Is America's Iniquity Full?," Apologetics Press, [On-line]: URL: http://www.apologeticspress.org/articles/305.

Miller, Dave (2006a), "Are Americans Abandoning God?," Apologetics Press, [On-line]: URL: http://www.apologeticspress.org/articles/3156.

Miller, Dave (2006b), *Sexual Anarchy* (Montgomery, AL: Apologetics Press).

Miller, Dave, et al. (2003), "An Investigation of the Biblical Evidence Against Homosexuality," *Reason & Revelation*, 24[9]:81, December, [On-line], URL: http://www.apologeticspress.org/articles/2577.

Miller, Sara B. (2003), "In Battle for Sunday, the 'Blue Laws' are Falling," *The Christian Science Monitor*, December 5, [On-line], URL: http://www.csmonitor.com/2003/1205/p01s02-usju.htm.

Mode, Peter G. (1921), *Sourcebook and Bibliographical Guide for American Church History* (Menasha, WI: George Banta Publishing).

Monaghan, Charles (2002), "Webster to McGuffey: A Sketch of American Literacy Textbooks," *History of Reading News*, Spring, [On-line], URL: http://www.historyliteracy.org/scripts/search_display.php?Article_ID=182.

Monaghan, E. Jennifer (1983), *A Common Heritage: Noah Webster's Blue-Back Speller* (Hamden, CT.: Archon Books).

Morison, Samuel (1935), *The Founding of Harvard* (Cambridge, MA: Harvard University Press).

Morris, Gouverneur (1821), "An Inaugural Discourse Delivered Before the New York Historical Society by the Honorable Gouverneur Morris on September 4, 1816" in *Collections of the New York Historical Society for the Year 1821* (New York: E. Bliss & E. White).

Morse, Jedidiah (1799), *A Sermon, Exhibiting the Present Dangers and Consequent Duties of the Citizens of the United States of America* (Hartford, CT: Hudson and Goodwin), [On-line]: URL: http://www.archive.org/details/sermonexhibiting00morsrich.

"Morse, Jedidiah" (2007), *Encyclopædia Britannica*, [On-line]: URL: http://www.britannica.com/eb/article-9053833.

New England Primer (1805), [On-line], URL: http://www.gettysburg.edu/~tshannon/his341/nep1805contents.html.

New Jersey State Constitution, [On-line], URL: http://www.njleg.state.nj.us/lawsconstitut ion/constitution.asp.

"The Nova Constellatio Patterns of 1783: Introduction" (no date), [On-line], URL: http://www.coins.nd.edu/ColCoin/ColCoinIntros/Nova Patterns.intro.html.

"On These Walls: Inscriptions and Quotations in the Buildings of the Library of Congress," Library of Congress, [On-line], URL: http://www. loc.gov/loc/walls/jeff1.html.

Paine, Robert Treat (1992), *The Papers of Robert Treat Paine*, ed. Stephen Riley and Edward Hanson (Boston, MA: Massachusetts Historical Society).

Palm, Daniel C. and Thomas L. Krannawitter (2004), "L.A. County's Seal and the Real Agenda of the ACLU," The Claremont Institute, [On-line], URL: http://www.claremont.org/writings/040609palm_kran.html.

"Patriotic Melodies," [On-line], URL: http://lcweb2.loc.gov/cocoon/ihas/loc.natlib.ihas.200000012/default.html.

People v. Ruggles, 8 Johns. 290 (N.Y. 1811).

Pierce, Benjamin (1833), *A History of Harvard University* (Cambridge, MA: Brown, Shattuck, & Co.).

"Politicians Fear Backlash from Gay 'Marriage'" (2004), *The Washington Times*, [On-line], URL: http://www.washtimes.com/national/20040222-122715-6305r.htm.

"Pony Express History" (no date), [On-line], URL: http://www.xphomestation.com/facts.html#J.

"President George Washington, 1789" (no date), Joint Congressional Committee on Inaugural Ceremonies, [On-line], URL: http://inaugural. senate.gov/history/chronology/gwashington1789.htm.

"Presidential Oaths of Office," Library of Congress, [On-line], URL: http://memory.loc.gov/ammem/pihtml/pioaths.htm.

Ramsay, David (1813), *An Eulogium Upon Benjamin Rush, M.D.* (Philadelphia, PA: Bradford & Inskeep).

Reagan, Ronald (1982), "Remarks at a White House Ceremony in Observance of National Day of Prayer," [On-line], URL: http://www.reagan. utexas.edu/archives/speeches/1982/50682c.htm.

"Relief Portraits of Lawgivers," The Architect of the Capitol, [On-line], URL: http://www.aoc.gov/cc/art/lawgivers/index.cfm.

"Religion and the Founding of the American Republic" (1998), Library of Congress, [On-line], URL: http://www.loc.gov/exhibits/religion/rel06.html.

Ringenberg, William C. (1984), *The Christian College: A History of Protestant Higher Education in America* (Grand Rapids, MI: Eerdmans).

Robinson, B.A. (2003), "Criminalizing Same-Sex Behavior," [On-line], URL: http://www.religioustolerance.org/hom_laws1.htm.

Roe v. Wade, 410 U.S. 113 (1973), [On-line], URL: http://caselaw.lp.findlaw.com/scripts/getcase.pl?court=US&vol=410&invol=113.

Roosevelt, Franklin (1941), "To the Congress of the United States," *Declarations of a State of War with Japan, Germany, and Italy: Part 3*, The Avalon Project at Yale Law School, [On-line], URL: http://www.yale.edu/lawweb/avalon/wwii/dec/dec03.htm#address.

Rowland, Kate (1892), *The Life of George Mason* (New York: G.P. Putnam's Sons).

"Royal Charter" (1693), The College of William and Mary, Earl Gregg Swem Library, Special Collections, [On-line], URL: http://swem.wm.edu/departments/special-collections/exhibits/exhibits/charter/charter/.

Runkel v. Winemiller, 4 H. & McH. 429; 1799 Md. LEXIS 43.

Rush, Benjamin (1798), *Essays, Literary, Moral and Philosophical* (Philadelphia, PA: Thomas & Samuel Bradford).

Rush, Benjamin (1951), *Letters of Benjamin Rush,* ed. L.H. Butterfield (Princeton, NJ: The American Philosophical Society).

Sanders, Jim (2003), "Controversy Erupts Over Landmark For Gay, Lesbian Soldiers," *Sacramento Bee*, Center for the Study of Sexual Minorities in the Military, University of California, Santa Barbara, [On-line], URL: http://www.gaymilitary.ucsb.edu/PressClips/03_0829_SacBee.htm.

Schlafly, Phyllis (2005), "Follies and Failures of the National Education Assn.," *The Phyllis Schlafly Report*, 39[1]:1, August, [On-line], URL: http://www.eagleforum.org/psr/2005/aug05/psraug05.html.

Smith, Gail (2000), "A Celebration of History," [On-line], URL: http://www.melbay.com/creativekeyboard/jul00/history.html.

Snyder, K. Alan (1990), *Defining Noah Webster: Mind and Morals in the Early Republic* (New York: University Press of America).

"Sodomy Laws in the United States" (2003), [On-line], URL: http://www.sodomylaws.org/usa/usa.htm.

Solenni, Pia de (2003), "Miracles of Life," *National Review Online*, September 30, [On-line], URL: http://www.nationalreview.com/comment/solenni200309301002.asp.

Sparks, Jared (1860), *Lives of William Pinkney, William Ellery, and Cotton Mather* (New York: Harper & Brothers).

"State Constitutions" (no date), The Avalon Project at Yale Law School, [On-line], URL: http://www.yale.edu/lawweb/avalon/states/stateco.htm.

"State Dining Room; Detail of Prayer Inscription of Fireplace Mantle, 376.118," Library of Congress, [On-line], URL: http://memory.loc.gov/

cgi-bin/displayPhoto.pl?path=/pnp/habshaer/dc/dc0400/dc0402/photos&topImages=026527pr.jpg&topLinks=026527pv.jpg,026527pu.tif&title=376.%20%20118%20State%20Dining%20Room;%20Detail%20of%20Prayer%20Inscription%20of%20Fire%20place%20Mantle%20%3Cbr%3EHABS%20DC,WASH,134-376&displayProfile=0.

"Statue of Liberty Inscriptions," [On-line], URL: http://www.nps.gov/history/history/online_books/hh/11/hh11q.htm.

Steiner, Bernard (1907), *The Life and Correspondence of James McHenry* (Cleveland, OH: Burrows Brothers).

Steiner, Bernard (1921), *One Hundred and Ten Years of Bible Society Work in Maryland: 1810-1920* (Baltimore, MD: Maryland Bible Society).

"The Story of American Public Education: Evolving Classroom" (2001), Alabama Public Television/PBS, [On-line], URL: http://www.pbs.org/kcet/publicschool/evolving_classroom/books.html.

Story, Joseph (1833), *Commentaries on the Constitution of the United States* (Boston, MA: Hilliard, Gray, & Co.), [On-line], URL: http://www.constitution.org/js/js_344.htm.

Summers, Lawrence (2002), "Commencement Address," Harvard University, June 6, [On-line], URL: http://www.president.harvard.edu/speeches/2002/commencement.html.

"Supreme Court Building," U.S. National Park Service, [On-line], URL: http://www.cr.nps.gov/history/online_books/butowsky2/constitution9.htm.

"Symbols of Law," [On-line], URL: http://www.supremecourtus.gov/about/symbolsoflaw.pdf.

"Symbols of U.S. Government: The Great Seal of the United States," [On-line], URL: http://bensguide.gpo.gov/3-5/symbols/seal.html.

Taylor, John (1970), *Garfield of Ohio: The Available Man* (New York: W.W. Norton).

"Thomas Jefferson Memorial: Statue Chamber Inscriptions," [On-line], URL: http://www.nps.gov/thje/memorial/inscript.htm.

Thompson, Parker (1978), *The United States Army Chaplaincy: from its European Antecedents to 1791* (Washington, DC: Office of the Chief of Chaplains, DOA).

Tocqueville, Alexis de (1835), *Democracy in America* (New York: Alfred Knopf, 1994 reprint).

"Tom Brokaw Books: The Greatest Generation," [On-line], URL: http://www.randomhouse.com/features/brokaw/books_greatest.html.

United States Code Online, [On-line], URL: http://usgovinfo.about.com/gi/dynamic/offsite.htm?site=http://www4.law.cornell.edu/uscode/.

The United States Constitution, [On-line], URL: http://www.house.gov/Constitution/Constitution.html.

United States v. Macintosh, 283 U.S. 605; 51 S. Ct. 570; 75 L. Ed. 1302; 1931 U.S. LEXIS 170.

"University Seal" (2002), GW News Center, Office of University Relations, The George Washington University, [On-line], URL: http://www.

gwu.edu/~newsctr/newscenter/guide/1_tour/armsandseal.html.

Updegraph v. the Commonwealth (1824), 11 Serg. & Rawle 394; 1824 Pa. LEXIS 85.

"U.S. Capitol Prayer Room" (no date), *Homeward Bound*, [On-line], URL: http://www.homewardboundjournal.com/2002/jan/special_feature.htm#gosee2.

U.S. Code (2002), [On-line], URL: http://frwebgate4.access.gpo.gov/cgi-bin/waisgate.cgi?WAISdocID=17233813733+1+0+0&WAISaction=retrieve.

"U.S. State Constitutions and Web Sites" (2003), [On-line], URL: http://www.constitution.org/cons/usstcons.htm.

Wallace v. Jaffree, 472 U.S. 38 (1985), [On-line], URL: http://caselaw.lp.findlaw.com/scripts/ff1#ff1.

Washington, George (1788), "George Washington to Benjamin Lincoln, June 29, 1788," George Washington Papers at the Library of Congress, 1741-1799, [On-line], URL: http://memory.loc.gov/cgi-bin/query/P?mgw:1:./temp/~ammem_iCgG::

Washington, George (1789), "First Inaugural Address," The Avalon Project at Yale Law School, [On-line], URL: http://www.yale.edu/lawweb/avalon/presiden/inaug/wash1.htm.

Washington, George (1796), "Farewell Address," The Avalon Project at Yale Law School, [On-line], URL: http://www.yale.edu/lawweb/avalon/washing.htm.

Washington, George (1838), *The Writings of George Washington*, ed. Jared Sparks (Boston, MA: American Stationers).

Washington, George (1932), *The Writings of Washington*, ed. John Fitzpatrick (Washington, DC: U.S. Government Printing Office).

"Washington Monument Memorial Stones," [On-line], URL: http://www.nps.gov/wamo/memstone2.htm.

"The Washington Monument Was Completed," [On-line], URL: http://www.americaslibrary.gov/cgi-bin/page.cgi/jb/gilded/monument_3.

Webster, Daniel (1903), *The Writings and Speeches of Daniel Webster* (Boston, MA: Little, Brown, & Co.).

Webster, Noah (1794), "The Revolution in France," in *Political Sermons of the American Founding Era: 1730-1805*, ed. Ellis Sandoz (Indianapolis, IN: Liberty Fund), 1998 edition, [On-line], URL: http://oll.libertyfund.org/title/817/69415.

Webster, Noah (1829), *The Elementary Spelling Book* (New York: American Book Company).

Webster, Noah (1832), *History of the United States* (New Haven, CT: Durrie & Peck).

Webster, Noah (1833), *The Holy Bible Containing the Old and New Testaments, in the Common Version. With Amendments of the Language* (New Haven, CT: Durrie & Peck).

Webster, Noah (1843), *A Collection of Papers on Political, Literary, and Moral Subjects* (New York: Webster & Clark).

Wirt, William (1818), *Sketches of the Life and Character of Patrick Henry* (Philadelphia, PA: James Webster).

Witherspoon, John (1802), *The Works of the Reverend John Witherspoon* (Philadelphia, PA: William Woodard).

Witherspoon, John (1815), *The Works of John Witherspoon* (Edinburgh: J. Ogle).

"Works of Art in the Capitol Complex," The Architect of the Capitol, [On-line], URL: http://www.aoc.gov/cc/art/index.cfm.

Yoffe, Emily (2000), "Can A President Change the Oath of Office?" [On-line], URL: http://slate.msn.com/id/1006398/.

AUTHOR'S NOTE

The term "Christian" is used accommodatively throughout this volume to refer to those who embrace the Christian worldview and the general principles of Christianity, in contradistinction to the non-Christian world religions (Hinduism, Buddhism, Islam, etc.) as well as irreligion (i.e., atheism, humanism, etc.). This use is commensurate with the sense employed by most of the global community. However, the term's pure, original sense is used in the New Testament to designate people who obeyed the gospel plan of salvation and practiced **un**denominational Christianity. For further information, visit www.ApologeticsPress. org and examine the free E-Book: *Receiving the Gift of Salvation*.